A FIRST CENTURY MESSAGE
TO
TWENTIETH CENTURY CHRISTIANS

A First Century Message
to
Twentieth Century Christians

*Addresses based upon the
Letters to the Seven Churches of Asia*

By
G. Campbell Morgan

Wipf & Stock
PUBLISHERS
Eugene, Oregon

Wipf and Stock Publishers
199 W 8th Ave, Suite 3
Eugene, OR 97401

A First Century Message to Twentieth Century Christians
Addresses based upon the Letters to the Seven Churches of Asia
By Morgan, G. Campbell
ISBN: 1-59244-805-4
Publication date 8/23/2004
Previously published by Fleming H. Revell Company, 1902

CONTENTS

		PAGE
I.	INTRODUCTORY	7
II.	THE VISION AND THE VOICE	15
III.	THE EPHESUS LETTER	31
IV.	THE SMYRNA LETTER	57
V.	THE PERGAMUM LETTER	83
VI.	THE THYATIRA LETTER	111
VII.	THE SARDIS LETTER	135
VIII.	THE PHILADELPHIA LETTER	159
IX.	THE LOADICEA LETTER	185

I

INTRODUCTORY

IN order to a proper understanding of the purpose of the letters to the churches of Asia, it is necessary that some word should be spoken concerning the book in which they are to be found.

This book contains the last messages of Christ to men. In some important ways it differs from any other in the Divine Library. John did not receive it by the inspiration of the Spirit in the ordinary sense of that expression, but directly from Jesus Christ, as He appeared to him while in exile in Patmos.

The usual title, "The Revelation of St. John, the Divine" is misleading, as the opening words of the book will show, which read, "The Revelation of Jesus Christ, which God gave Him to show unto His servants." Perhaps no book has been more neglected than this Revelation of Jesus Christ, and yet it the only one that opens with a distinct and three-fold blessing pronounced, a blessing first, upon those who read, secondly, upon those who hear, thirdly, upon those who keep the things that are written therein.

There must be some deep significance in this introductory pronouncement, and because of the difficulty of interpretation, the Church has no right to neglect her Master's last message.

Yet while it is true that no book has been so sadly neglected, it is also true that around no book has there waged more persistent controversy. So keen has that controversy been, that we find Christian people divided into distinct schools of thought about it, and we hear of Preterist, Presentist, Futurist, and Spiritual interpretations. These differences have no detailed place in our present discussion. Our business lies only with the messages to the churches. That we may see their place, some word must be said about the general character of the book.

The book of Revelation is not primarily a book of Church truth. It is a book of judgment in the broadest sense of that word, judgment, that is, as the method and government of God. It reveals the consummation of the world's history, and gives a panorama of God's final dealings with the earth. We find ourselves largely back in the realm of Old Testament truth. Jehovah is introduced in language in keeping with the thoughts suggested by that name to the ancient Hebrew people, "Him which is and which was and which is to come." The Holy Spirit is spoken of, not as the unified personality that men came to know through the work of Christ, and Who appears in the Epistles of the New Testament. He is seen rather as seven Spirits, that is, in the perfection of activity, and these Spirits, moreover, are before the throne. Jesus is the "faithful Witness, the First-born from the dead, and the Ruler of the kings of the earth;" while the Church, loved and loosed from sin, is a kingdom of priests, perfected in their number, and save in the early chapters, occupying a place in glory. Thus God is revealed as supreme in the government of the universe, the Spirit as the light and activity of that government, and Jesus as the faithful Witness, and as ruling the kings of the earth.

The outlook of Revelation is larger than the Church of Christ. It deals, not with the relation of God as Father to the company of saved in the Church, but to His larger relation as King and Governor of the whole earth. There has been a great deal of cloudy thinking and teaching on these subjects. Many seem to imagine that the Church and the Kingdom of God are one and the same thing. The fact is that the Kingdom of God is infinitely larger than the Church, and includes that whole realm over which God is King, and in which that Kingship will finally be established. To-day the Church recognizes and submits to that Kingship. The time will come when all nations shall recognize and submit. The Church is an instrument to that end. And yet she is a complete entity within herself, having her specific vocation in future ages.

The whole book of Revelation reveals the final stages in the work of God with humanity. No one has perfectly understood all its teaching. Its great principles are evident. It shows the final overthrow of evil, and the setting up of the eternal Kingdom of God. It moreover teaches us that that overthrow and that setting up will be realized through Jesus the anointed King.

In all probability the key to the division of the book is to be found in the words, "Write therefore the things which thou sawest, and the things which are, and the things which shall come to pass hereafter." This verse divides the book, and marks the subjects upon which John was commissioned by Jesus to write.

Introductory

i. "The things which thou sawest."
ii. "The things which are."
iii. "The things which shall come to pass after these."

The first of these undoubtedly has reference to the vision of glory that John looked upon, the second to the condition of things existent as described in the seven letters to the churches, and the things "after these" are the final things, the chronicle of which commences in chapter iv, verse 1. Let it be noted that in chapter i, verse 19, the word "hereafter" is a translation of the two words μετὰ ταῦτα, and in chapter iv, verse 1, "after these things" is a translation of the same two words. Thus evidently the third division begins at the fourth chapter, and from there to the end we have unfulfilled prophecy. With this section of the book we have now nothing to do. Our particular subject is the second division, "the things which are."

Of this there have been three interpretations. First, that the epistles were actually written to seven churches at the time existing in Asia. Second, that the epistles contain an unfolding of the condition of the Church in successive stages of its history. Third, that the epistles give a picture of seven conditions of Church life to be found continuously in the history of the Church of Christ. My own conviction is that all these are true. I propose however, to consider them in the light of the first and third, that is to say, as letters written to actual churches, and as having perpetual application to some phase of Church life. While there is very little doubt that they do reveal a process in the history of the Church, upon that phase of their teaching I do not intend to touch.

We shall first look at the vision which arrested John in the Isle of Patmos, then at the seven epistles, endeavouring to gather their message to the age in which we live; so that we are to give attention to a first century message to twentieth century Christians.

In dealing with each of the epistles, we shall notice four distinct matters,

    i. Christ's title.
    ii. Christ's commendation.
    iii. Christ's complaint.
    iv. Christ's counsel.

These will not always be in this exact order, for in some cases either commendation or complaint is omitted, but for these as main points of interest we shall look in our studies.

THE VISION AND THE VOICE

"And I turned to see the voice which spake with me. And having turned I saw seven golden lampstands; and in the midst of the lampstands One like unto a Son of man, clothed with a garment down to the foot, and girt about at the breasts with a golden girdle. And His head and His hair were white as white wool, white as snow; and His eyes were as a flame of fire; and His feet like unto burnished brass, as if it had been refined in a furnace; and His voice as the voice of many waters. And He had in His right hand seven stars: and out of His mouth proceeded a sharp two-edged sword: and His countenance was as the sun shineth in his strength."

. . . .,

"The mystery of the seven stars which thou sawest in My right hand, and the seven golden lampstands. The seven stars are the angels of the seven churches: and the seven lampstands are seven churches." — Rev. i: 12-16, 20.

II

THE VISION AND THE VOICE

WHEN in the loneliness of Patmos John heard a voice behind him, he "turned to see . . . and having turned he saw." The vision that fell upon him was present during all the messages he received for the churches, lending value and emphasis to these messages. If we therefore are to understand, we also must see the vision. Let us take a general survey, note the first impression produced, and then proceed to a careful examination of the central figure.

"Having turned he saw seven golden lampstands. . . . One like unto a Son of man. . . . He had in His right hand seven stars." He first beheld seven golden lampstands. "Lampstand" is a better translation, and far more perfectly conveys the true symbolism. A candlestick presupposes a kind of light which is self-consumptive. A lampstand presupposes a light which may be perpetually fed by oil, and in Scripture, oil is constantly emblematic of the Holy Spirit. Of these lampstands the Master

Himself gives the interpretation. "The seven lampstands are seven churches." Thus each individual church is seen as a centre of light.

Then "in the midst of the lampstands" he saw "One like unto a Son of man." Thus Christ is seen in all human sympathy, presiding over the churches in the exercise of their function.

He moreover notices that in the right hand of the Son of man were seven stars, and here again we have the interpretation of the Lord, "The seven stars are the angels of the seven churches."

The first impression produced by the vision is peculiar, and apparently contradictory. It is evidently a night scene, as witness the lampstands and the stars, and yet it is a day scene, for behold, the countenance of the Son of man is "as the sun shineth in his strength." John beheld as in a vision, the Church in its present relation and responsibility to Christ and the world. The night all around is the world's darkness. The only light shining upon that darkness is that which comes from the lampstands. The vision of Christ's face as that of the sun, is a revelation of what He is to His people. To them it is day time. "For ye are all sons of light, and sons of the day: we are

The Vision and the Voice

not of the night, nor of darkness." The Church is here seen as the light bearer, with Christ as unifying Centre and directing Authority. Christ Himself in the midst of the seven lampstands creates their unity. The unity of the Church consists in the common relationship of each church to the Lord Himself Who is present in the midst.

In His right hand He holds the messengers, and herein is revealed the true position that ministry occupies in the Christian Church, whether it be the ministry of authoritative teaching as given through the apostles, the ministry of prophetic utterance, the ministry of evangelization, or that of the pastoral office. Christ the truth, the angel His messenger, the Church that to which truth is made known by the messenger, and in which truth is embodied, that its light may fall upon the surrounding darkness. No man can be a messenger of the Master and the Church save as he is held in the right hand of Jesus, and interprets, not his own idea concerning the Church's wellbeing, nor the Church's wish concerning its function, but the will of the Master. The messenger has no authority in himself, no authority which he derives from the Church over which he presides. His authority is the communicated authority of the Son of man, Who is Lord and Master of the whole.

In the midst of the world's night, the Church unified by the presence of the Lord, diversified in the seven lampstands, is a light shining in a dark place. This perfectly sets forth the one responsibility of every church of Jesus Christ. It is to be a medium through which the essential Light of the world shall shine upon the world's darkness. A most important principle to be perpetually borne in mind by those who would fulfil the highest function of Church life is that the world waits for light, and the Church's only capacity for shedding the light, is that she should live in the day which the face of Christ creates for her. No church and no individual member of a church, can fling across the darkness one ray or gleam of light save as that church or that person lives in the sunshine created by the shining of His face. When the Master was here He said " I am the Light of the world." That Light was eclipsed in the darkness of Calvary's Cross, but from behind the dense cloud, it broke again to shine upon all those who receive life by the way of that Cross, and through them to flash upon the night of the world.

Thus having seen the general scheme, before

The Vision and the Voice

passing to a close consideration of the central Figure, we pause for a moment to look again at the lampstands and at the stars.

Let it be emphasized that the lampstands are not the sources of light but the bearers of light, also that their number is seven, and that they are golden. So that if they do not in themselves create light, it is evident that the medium upon which the light is to rest, and from which it is to flash upon the darkness, must be heavenly and perfect. While we have no light of our own with which to help men in the darkness, for God's light must shine upon and through us, we must in order to that shining, know what it is to partake of that nature which is symbolized by the gold of the sanctuary. Thus we have a symbolism of function, and a symbolism of character.

The stars held in His right hand are symbols of the fact that ministry to be effective, must be of heavenly character, revolving solely around the central sun.

In reverently examining the central figure, we notice first His position. He is "in the midst of the lampstands," unifying them into one whole, and directing them by individual messages, showing His intimate acquaintance with the details of each.

His general appearance is that of the Son of man. It is important to remember that this phrase occurs in the Gospel narratives with regard to the Master, eighty-five times, and of these, Christ Himself makes use of it eighty-three. The first detail of the vision is a symbolism of function, and the second a symbolism of character.

His function is suggested by His robing. "Clothed with a garment down to the foot, and girt about at the breasts with a golden girdle." Two things are suggested by this double figure. The garment to the foot suggests the right to govern and to judge. It is the robing of judicial authority, not the robing of the priest. He is here seen as the central Authority in all Church life, having sole right to pronounce verdict and sentence upon all the service that the Church renders. The girdle is frequently mentioned in Scripture. Sometimes it is the girdle of the loins, and sometimes the girdle of the breasts. The former is the symbol of activity and power, the latter that of faithfulness and affection. In this case the girdle is at the breasts, showing the fidelity of His love. This robing of the Son of Man reveals His judicial position

The Vision and the Voice

among the churches, and that all the exercise of judicial right is based upon the faithfulness of the Eternal Love.

A remarkable Scripture in the prophecy of Isaiah will serve to throw light upon the robing. "And it shall come to pass in that day, that I will call My servant Eliakim the son of Hilkiah: and I will clothe him with Thy robe, and strengthen him with Thy girdle, and I will commit Thy government into his hand: and he shall be a father to the inhabitants of Jerusalem, and to the house of Judah." There is of course no immediate connection between the subject dealt with in Isaiah and the one now under consideration, but we refer to it that we may have light upon the symbolism of the robe and the girdle in our vision.

Jesus moves amid the churches with the robe reaching to His feet, marking the fact that He is the sole Governor of His people, having the right to pass His verdict upon their service, and reward or punish them as He will. The golden girdle about the breasts reveals the fact that every judgment He pronounces, and every sentence He passes, is based upon His infinite love and faithfulness. Christ is the one supreme Head, Ruler, Governor, among His people, and all His headship, and His rule, and His government are based upon His infinite and unfailing compassion.

Passing from the symbolism of function to that of character we have the most marvellous and entrancing vision of Jesus Christ contained in Scripture. We can do no more than pass rapidly over, attempting to indicate the significance of the sevenfold glory revealed.

"His head and His hair were white as white wool, white as snow."

"His eyes were as a flame of fire."

"His feet like unto burnished brass, as if it had been refined in a furnace."

"His voice as the voice of many waters."

"In His right hand seven stars."

"Out of His mouth proceeded a sharp two-edged sword."

"His countenance was as the sun shineth in his strength."

Here are seven points to which our attention is directed. His head, His hair, His eyes, His feet, His voice, His hand, His mouth, His countenance.

Let us take them in their order.

"*His head and His hair were white as white wool, white as snow.*" Two facts are symbolized by this language, His purity and His eternity. The description is remarkably similar to that in the book of Daniel, describing the "Ancient of Days." The hair white as wool is the mark of age, and yet of age that is not aged. This whiteness is moreover the symbol of purity, and these two facts are, in the last analysis, but one, for all eternal things are pure, and only purity can be eternal. The doomed things are the base, the impure, the unholy things, and in the glorious vision of the royal head of the Son of man, shining like some snow-capped mountain peak, far elevated, we see Him as Son of God also, His purity the basis of His eternity, His eternity the crowning of His purity.

"*His eyes were as a flame of fire.*" Here the suggestion is that of infinite and infallible knowledge, eyes that pierce and penetrate, from which no secret thing can possibly be hidden, eyes that being as a flame of fire, seeing through and through, detect all that is hidden from ordinary sight, separating with unerring accuracy the alloy from the pure gold. Thus the Son of man amid the churches is revealed as the One from Whom nothing can be hidden. There is no detail in the doings of a church, or in the life of an individual member, that He is not perfectly acquainted with. He has seen and rightly valued every deed of lowly service which the earthly records of the Church have found no place for. The steady, searching eyes of the great Son of man are ever upon the churches that bear His name, and absolutely nothing can be hidden from that gaze.

"*His feet like unto burnished brass, as if it had been refined in a furnace.*" The feet are the symbols of procedure, and indicate the continued activity of Christ among the churches, and through the churches, as He marches, the Leader of the hosts of God, toward His ultimate victory.

These feet are of brass as though they burned in a furnace. Brass is invariably the type of strength, and the furnace of fire is symbolic of purification. Thus the Son of man is seen moving amid the churches ever toward the consummation upon which the heart of God is set, with such absolute purity, that He can never be contaminated with the evil upon which He treads, and with such tremendous strength that He can never be prevented by the opposition raised against Him.

"*His voice as the voice of many waters.*" This exquisitely beautiful statement I think I never appreciated until for the first time I stood near the mighty falls of Niagara, as the water sweeps from height to depth in calm persistent majesty with a cry that excludes all other sounds, possesses all your soul, and yet fills you with a deep peace and quiet. The mighty music of the many waters impressed me as nothing else, and as I listened there came to me with new meaning the words " His voice as the voice of many waters."

The suggestion is very beautiful. What is the voice of many waters? It is a perfect concord of divers tones; many waters, one voice. " God, having of old time spoken unto the fathers in the prophets by divers portions and in divers manners, hath at the end of these days spoken unto us in His Son." " His voice as the voice of many waters." These waters have come from the hills of long ago in single streams, all their courses bent toward Him. In Him they mingle and they merge, and in Him is discovered the perfect harmony of the thousand melodies of the past. Close attention by a trained ear will detect each separate value, and it will be found that there is no subject upon which He has not something to say. He speaks to art, to music, to science, to literature, to all life, to each separately, and yet to each in its relation to all the rest. Many waters, many messengers, many messages, yet one voice, one word, one revelation.

So moving amid the lampstands, with hair like wool, telling of His purity and eternity, with eyes as a flame of fire, searching and knowing every detail of all the life of the churches, with His feet like brass that burned in a furnace, moving toward the consummation, He speaks, and the infinite music is a perfect harmony of all the tones of the voice of God.

"*He had in His right hand seven stars.*" In all the symbolism of the old economy, the right hand is the mark of authoritative administration, and here has the same significance. In the centre of that hand of power rest the seven stars which are the angels of the churches, the place of perfect rest, perfect power, perfect protection. Oh, blessed, blessed place of rest for the Master's messengers! Oh, high and holy honour to lie in that right hand, and listen while He speaks, and still from the same vantage ground to repeat the words of His will.

"*Out of His mouth proceeded a sharp two-edged sword.*" We have heard the voice of many waters that speaks of revelation, of His uttering of the deep things of God. Here is

The Vision and the Voice 27

symbolized another aspect of His speech to men, that namely of His pronouncement on the things of men. While He was yet on earth, He distinctly affirmed that by His words men should be judged, and the value of this symbolism will be better understood as we hear His verdicts concerning the churches amid whom He moves. It will then be seen how sharp that sword is, and how its double action condemns the fault and approves the excellence.

" His countenance as the sun shineth in his strength." The countenance is the sum total of all the features of the face. The dome-like splendour of the forehead, crowned by the white hair, the flashing glory of the wondrous eyes, the marvellous expressiveness of the mouth, from which proceeds the sword-like speech, and the sound of the voice of many waters; take all these, and other things not described, in combination, and the result is a sun of light and glory, shining in strength. " God is a sun," and the merging of the features of humanity into the perfect impression of the countenance, reveals in might and majesty the Deity of the Son of man.

Take this picture and look at it again and again until the vision holds you in its marvellous power. His head and His hair white like wool, His purity and His eternity; His eyes like a flame of fire, His intimate knowledge, penetrating and piercing; His feet like burnished brass, signifying the procedure of strength and purity; His voice like the voice of many waters, a concord of perfect tones; in His hand seven stars, His administrative right, power and protection; from His mouth a sharp two-edged sword, keen and accurate verdicts concerning His people; His whole countenance as the sun, creating day, flashing light, bathing all the landscape with beauty.

Such was the One Who moved amid the churches in the vision of the saint at Patmos, and such the One who still unifies the churches into the Church, by His presence and presidence.

Thus the Lord is seen in all the fulness and the functions of His glory, presiding over the witnessing of the Church in the midst of darkness, and we now turn to a study of the messages He delivers, ever keeping this vision before us.

THE EPHESUS LETTER

"To the angel of the church in Ephesus write;

"These things saith He that holdeth the seven stars in His right hand, He that walketh in the midst of the seven golden lampstands: I know thy works, and thy toil and patience, and that thou canst not bear evil men, and didst try them which call themselves apostles, and they are not, and didst find them false; and thou hast patience and didst bear for My name's sake, and hast not grown weary. But I have against thee, that thou didst leave thy first love. Remember therefore from whence thou art fallen, and repent, and do the first works; or else I come to thee, and will move thy lampstand out of its place, except thou repent. But this thou hast, that thou hatest the works of the Nicolaitans, which I also hate. He that hath an ear, let him hear what the Spirit saith to the churches. To him that overcometh, to him will I give to eat of the tree of life, which is in the Paradise of God." Rev. ii: 1-7.

III

THE EPHESUS LETTER

AT the time of the writing of the epistle, Ephesus was the metropolis of Ionia, and undoubtedly a great and opulent city. All kinds of people were gathered there, the wealthy and the learned, as well as the poor and the illiterate. The general condition of life was that of a wealthy, cultured, and corrupt community.

So far as the history of the church is concerned, we have a most interesting account of its planting and progress in the Acts of the Apostles. This account lies almost completely within chapters eighteen to twenty. Paul on his journeyings arrived in the city accompanied by Aquila and Priscilla. As his custom was, he went into the synagogue, and spoke to the assembled people of the one theme ever on his heart. Passing on his way, he left behind him these two people. Thus was first spoken the message of the risen and crucified Christ, and from such an apparently hurried commencement there came eventually a strong and remarkable church.

The next event of note was the arrival of Apollos. He had learned of Jesus through the ministry of John, and was a man of splendid mental equipment and great oratorical power. In Ephesus he declared all he knew of truth with the result that a little group of men, attracted by the story he had to tell, imperfect though it was, were baptized with the baptism of John. Beyond that they made no progress. They were in all about twelve in number.

Then came a crisis. Paul returned to Ephesus, Apollos having passed on to Achaia and Corinth. In the nineteenth and twentieth chapters of the Acts we have, briefly stated, the work he accomplished during a period of about three years. It is very interesting to notice the growth. He found twelve disciples, imperfectly instructed, not yet having received the Spirit of God, men who were followers of Christ so far as they had light. Apollos had preached the baptism of water to repentance as preparatory to entrance upon the Kingdom over which Jesus was to preside. Paul found them ignorant of the very essentials of Christianity, and asked them evidently in a tone of surprise and enquiry, "Did ye receive the Holy Ghost when ye believed." And they replied "Nay, we did not as much as hear

The Ephesus Letter 33

whether the Holy Ghost was given." This called for further enquiry as to the nature of their baptism, and then finding that they had been baptized with John's baptism, he led them into further light. How much they had gained from obedience to the light received is revealed by their readiness to obey the new light that fell. They were baptized into the name of the Lord Jesus, and the apostle, laying his hands upon them, they received the Holy Spirit.

Then Paul began to teach in the synagogue, and it is a remarkable fact that they suffered him to do this for three months. The effect of the preaching was as always. To those who were disobedient there came hardness, and a spirit of opposition was aroused. The apostle saw that the time had arrived for the outward formation of a church. He gathered the disciples out of the synagogue, and securing the school of Tyrannus, he began preaching there. During two years the church grew until it became a great centre of missionary operations. The Word of God sounded out through all Asia as the result of the teaching in Ephesus.

Then mark what followed. Imitators arose, men desiring to accomplish the same results, but lacking the necessary power. Some of these took upon themselves the work of casting out evil spirits, using the name of Jesus saying, "I adjure you by Jesus Whom Paul preacheth." But demons were not so to be deceived, and the startling answer came "Jesus I know, and Paul I know; but who are ye? And the man in whom the evil spirit was, leaped on them, and mastered both of them, and prevailed against them, so that they fled out of that house naked and wounded."

Attempts to imitate the work of the Spirit through the servants of God always ends disastrously to those who make the attempt. From this experience the work blazed out again in new power. Fear fell upon all, and those that practiced magical arts, brought their books together and burned them.

Then followed new opposition against Paul, the reason being that he had endangered the craftsmen's art.

Then Paul left Ephesus, and journeyed through Macedonia. Passing back through the same region, he paused at Miletus that he might there meet the elders of the church at Ephesus, and as he was to be no more with them, he gave them parting instructions.

It is more than probable that at this time John came down and took oversight of the

The Ephesus Letter

church. How long he remained it is impossible to decide. In all likelihood the message of Jesus to the church of Ephesus was sent about thirty-five years after Paul's departure. It reveals the changes that had been wrought. To it we now turn our attention.

The Lord introduces Himself as "He that holdeth the seven stars in His right hand, He that walketh in the midst of the seven golden lampstands." Here as always there is a very remarkable fitness of selection. It is evident that the church at Ephesus is fulfilling the true ideal of Church order. Christ is seen as the unifying Centre and Director of the church, walking still amid the seven golden lampstands, and holding in His right hand the seven stars. No other things in that descriptive vision are mentioned concerning Him. The true Church order is still maintained, the ministry is in its proper and rightful place. Outwardly everything is as it should be. There is no flaw, no failure, in organization, in work, in attitude, so far as any visiting apostle could have discovered it, or so far as the world was concerned in watching it.

Then follows our Lord's commendation, a commendation so remarkable that I venture to think a careful consideration of it will leave us inclined to ask, Can there be anything wrong with this church? Had we visited it, in all probability we should have reported that it was the most remarkable church we had ever seen. The commendation is sevenfold. " I know thy works, and thy toil and patience, and that thou canst not bear evil men, and didst try them which call themselves apostles, and they are not, and didst find them false; and thou hast patience and didst bear for My name's sake, and hast not grown weary." One is startled at the completeness of the commendation. Consider it closely.

" I know thy works." This has reference to actual service being rendered. The church was not a comfortable club for the conserving of the life of a few saints. It was an active and aggressive congregation of the saints.

" I know thy toil." This word lies deeper, having reference to the effort that produces work even at the cost of pain. There are those who boast that their work and their gifts cost them nothing. Wherever that is true the work is worthless. These people at Ephesus could make no such boast, for behind the works lay the toil. They were not offering to the Master, to the church, to the world things worthless because costless. They were working at the price of toil.

"And thy patience," that is the attitude of persistence in the toil that produces the work. These first three words are closely linked,— "works, toil, patience." And the words are the more wonderful as we remember they fall from the lips of Jesus. It is not merely the opinion of an apostle or a stranger. It is the definitely expressed verdict of the Lord of the church, the One Who with eyes of fire, scans every detail. I know your works, and that behind them there is the toil that speaks of pain, and enveloping that there is the patient endurance that makes work perpetual.

And "I know that thou canst not bear evil men." There is no impurity condoned within the borders of this church. It has no complicity with the evil things in Ephesus. They had guarded the fellowship of the saints against the unholy intrusion of impure men. They had not been lax in their discipline as to life.

"Thou didst try them which call themselves apostles, and they are not, and didst find them false." The church had been careful about its doctrine, careful about what it listened to, characterized by discernment and judgment of false teachers. Not only had their discipline been perfect as to the life of their members, but they had refused to tolerate the false teachers that had come to them.

And yet again "Thou hast patience and didst bear for My name's sake." Their persistent fidelity had not been in circumstances that were always easy. Persecution had raged around them, and yet they had maintained their works.

And then the last and most remarkable word, "Thou hast not grown weary." They had a great reserve of strength. All the achievements had been under the impulse of, and in the power of unswerving fidelity.

This description is surely most remarkable. The church at work, labouring at the work, patiently persistent in the labour that produced the work. The church refusing to have fellowship with evil men, observing the false philosophy of certain teaching and rejecting it. The church, persistent in its faithfulness and unwearying in its service. If the Master, visiting the church to which we belong uttered such words as these, should we not feel that they constituted the highest commendation that could possibly be passed?

And yet once again, after the complaint which He makes, He adds something more to the commendation. "But this thou hast, that thou hatest the works of the Nicolaitans, which I also hate." Some doubt exists as to the peculiar views of the Nicolaitans. Some light may be thrown upon the subject by reference to the letter to Pergamum. "I have a few things against thee, because thou hast there some that hold the teaching of Balaam, who taught Balak to cast a stumblingblock before the children of Israel, to eat things sacrificed to idols, and to commit fornication. So hast thou also some that hold the teaching of the Nicolaitans in like manner." My personal conviction is that the Nicolaitans were persons who excused certain forms of impurity, and made the grace of God a cloak for lasciviousness. I believe the heresy was that known in latter days as Antinomianism, which declares that grace is sufficient for salvation, and that life is of little moment. This heresy will be dealt with more fully in considering the letter to Pergamum.

So wonderful a commendation seems to leave nothing to be desired. No eye but the penetrating eye of fire which is the eye of love would ever have detected the failure of the church at Ephesus, at this point. Subsequently that failure would have been detected even by the outsider. The living Lord was conscious of the incipient disease which others could only know as it manifested itself in the externalities. Light focussed in a camera has revealed the presence of disease in the face of a child long before any symptoms appeared which a physician could have detected. So the searching light of the eyes of fire detected the absence of an essential quality in the life of the church.

"I have against thee, that thou didst leave thy first love." That is all. No other sentence. No other word. Immediately He passes to the counsel which He has to give to the church. And yet how much He has said. Seeing the church now in the light of His declaration, all the radiance of the former things is over-shadowed. What is first love, and what is it to lose first love?

First love is the love of espousal. First love is marital. In writing to the Corinthian church, Paul said, " For I espoused you to one husband, that I might present you as a pure virgin to Christ. But I fear, lest by any means, as the serpent beguiled Eve in his craftiness, your minds should be corrupted

The Ephesus Letter 41

from the simplicity and the purity that is toward Christ." That is first love. "I espoused you to one husband, that I might present you as a pure virgin to Christ." And this is the loss of pure love. "But I fear, lest by any means, as the serpent beguiled Eve in his craftiness, your minds should be corrupted from the simplicity and the purity that is toward Christ." The elements of first love then are simplicity and purity. Now think for a moment of what this same man wrote to this church at Ephesus. After dealing with the relation of husbands to wives, and wives to husbands, he pens this marvellous statement, "This mystery is great: but I speak in regard of Christ and of the Church."

Now what is the mystery to which he refers. It is the mystery of love which has its most radiant revelation in the marriage relationship, and the apostle declares that that relationship is the most perfect symbol of that existing between Christ and His Bride. "Husbands, love your wives, even as Christ also loved the Church." Thus it is evident that Christ's love for the Church is typified by the love of husband for wife. "Wives, be in subjection unto your own husbands, as unto the Lord." Thus the love of the Church to Christ is typified by the love of the wife for the husband. What then is the love of Christ to the Church? Unselfish love, love in which there was no single thought of self. What then is the Church's love for Christ? The response of love to the mystery of love, the submission of love to perfect love. First love is the love of espousal. Its notes are simplicity, and purity, marital love, the response of love to love, the subjection of a great love to a great love, the submission of a self-denying love to a love that denies self. First love is the abandonment of all for a love that has abandoned all.

First love defies analysis. It loves, it knows not why, save that the lover has by love attracted love, and the responsive love is pure, unselfish, ardent, humble. The church at Ephesus had had its first love, the love of espousal, the love of simplicity, the love of singleness, the love in which no low motive lurked. First love is fair as the morning, bright with the promise of hope, a flame in the presence of which all other emotions and enthusiasms are included. It was this the Master missed. No soul can try to love Him. When you felt your need of Him as Saviour, and there dawned upon you the vision of His perfect love, and you found that the perfect sal-

The Ephesus Letter

vation He offered was Himself given to you, your raptured soul was bound to Him by the excellency of His own character. In the consciousness of the infinite love of His heart your love was born, and the first flush of that young love of yours was pure, unselfish, humble, ardent, burning like a flame, consuming everything in its fervour and its fire.

Now think of the infinite pathos of that one sentence of complaint. "Thou didst leave thy first love." The emotion and the enthusiasm and the energy are lacking. Jesus recognizes this. Had Judas been a member of this church, he would have found nothing to criticize. He criticized Mary of Bethany, and why? Because the love of Mary of Bethany was the love that overstepped all the bounds of prudence and regularity. Love cannot be weighed in scales or measured with a foot rule. It overleaps the channel you cut for it, and laughs its way into meadows, leaving behind it the track of fertility and the fragrance of flowers. You cannot compress it into mathematical formulæ. It sings in poetry, and forgets calculation. It worships in abandonment, and oversteps arithmetic. It is a vestal flame. It is the crowning consciousness of life.

The church at Ephesus was still a remarkable church, but it lacked the element of that enthusiasm, which in the eyes of the calculating worldling, is imprudent. There are some people who imagine that this lack of enthusiasm is an advantage. May God have mercy on such. I pray the day may never come when the heroisms and enthusiasms of first love shall cease. Christ stands confronting this great church, and He says in effect, There is much of excellency, but I miss the first love. I do not hear the song at the unusual hour. I wait in vain for the aroma of some new box of spikenard. The church has become

> "Faultily faultless, icily regular,
> Splendidly null."

After Christ has spoken, we begin to reconsider the commendation, and even in that commendation now it is possible to detect omissions, things He did not say which He might have said, had they not left their first love.

In Paul's first letter to the Thessalonians we have inferentially a picture of a church in its first love. There were many irregularities of doctrine and of conduct, but there was a great enthusiasm. The apostle describing their condition says, "Remembering without ceasing

The Ephesus Letter 45

your work of faith and labour of love and patience of hope in our Lord Jesus Christ."

Here are the same things that Christ commends in Ephesus and yet how different. In the full rush of first love the apostle says of the Thessalonians " work of faith . . . labour of love . . . patience of hope." But speaking to the church at Ephesus Jesus says " work . . . labour . . . patience." What are the missing things? " The faith, the love, the hope." In first love it is " work of faith." First love lost, it is " work." In first love it is " labour of love." First love lost, it is " labour." In first love it is " patience of hope." With first love lost it is " patience." The externalities remain, but the underlying sources have been weakened. Faith, out of which work grows, is faltering. Love, the principle of toil, is waning. Hope, the inspiration of perpetual patience, is dimmed. Now these three, faith, hope, and love alike centre in the Person. Where faith in Him is strong, works abide. Where love for Him is full, enduring toil continues. Where hope toward Him is perfect, patience is perpetual. As yet the outward manifestations are not, but the Master has discovered the inward backsliding. He says in effect, You have lost your first love, your works run on, but your faith in Me is not what it was, your labour is still evident, but the love is weakened; your patience is still evident, but your hope does not burn so brightly. And presently He will mark the full meaning of this. Unless you repent and get back to these first things, you will lose your lampstand. When the flame of love flickers, then its sisters, faith and hope grow faint, and presently the outward light will burn low, and the surrounding darkness be unilluminated.

In the light of these statements moreover, other parts of the commendation may be reconsidered. Is it not more than likely that their very opposition to false men and doctrine partook of the nature of lack of love? I would speak very cautiously at this point, for the Lord commended these things, and they were right, but I am quite sure that there may be right things done in a wrong spirit. I seldom find men strenuously fighting what they are pleased to call heterodox teaching, and in bitter language denouncing false doctrine, without being more afraid for the men denouncing than for the men denounced. There is an anger against impurity which is impure. There is a zeal for orthodoxy which is most unorthodox.

The Ephesus Letter 47

There is a spirit that contends for faith which is in conflict with faith. If men have lost their first love, they will do more harm than good by their defence of the faith. Behind the denunciation of sin there must always be the tenderness of first love if that denunciation is not to become evil in its bitterness. Behind the zeal for truth, there must always be the spaciousness of first love if that zeal is not to become narrowed into hate. There have been men who have become so self-centred in a narrowness that they are pleased to designate as holding the truth, that the very principle for which they contend has been excluded from their life and service. All zeal for the Master that is not the outcome of love to Him is worthless. His love is so perfect that nothing can take the place of love as a return. He who woos the bride can never have his heart satisfied with a servant. Activity in the King's business will not make up for neglect of the King. He who has lost his first love cannot satisfy with work and labour and patience, and hatred of sin and orthodoxy. The Master waits for love. Your church may pass muster as one of those amid which He walks; but He, walking there pines for your love, and nothing satisfies Him but love. Oh the pathos of the picture! Christ in all His glory seeks amid the churches first for love. As He looks over the outward perfections of Ephesus He discovers that the spirit, the tone, the temper of the church is altered. No eye but His could have detected that the bloom was brushed away, and that the flame was less ardent.

Surely this message needs to be repeated to all our churches to-day. Your work, your labour, your patience are all evident. Never were you busier. Never were your organizations more complete, but where is your first love? A friend of mine some years ago had a little daughter whom he dearly loved, and at the time of my story, she was between ten and eleven years of age. They were great friends, and were always found in each other's company. But about this time there seemed to come some estrangement between them for which he could not account. He was not able to get her company as he had been. She seemed to shun him, and if he went for a walk, excused herself for she had something she must do at home. He grieved about it and could not understand it, and yet hardly cared to mention to her what was apparent to him. One day his birthday came, and in the morning of that day she came into his room, with her face wreathed in smiles and said "Father I have brought you a present." She handed him a parcel, and unfastening it he found an exquisitely worked pair of slippers. He said "Darling, it was very good of you to buy these for me." "Oh, Father," said she, "I did not buy them. I have made them for you." Then looking at her he said "Oh, now I think I understand. Is this what you have been doing for the last three months?" She replied "Yes, Father, but how did you know how long I had been at work on them?" He said "Because for three months I have wanted much of you, but have not been able to have it. You have been too busy. My darling, I like these slippers very much, but next time, buy the slippers, and let me have you all the days, I would rather have my child than anything she can make for me."

That story has ever been weighted for me with spiritual value. Some of us are so busy here and there about the business of the Lord that He cannot get us much for Himself. There is so much to be done. Do not misunderstand me. We are perfectly sincere in our devotion, and yet it seems to me as if sometimes He would say "I know your works, your labour, your patience, but I miss the first love." Do you not remember your first love, with its great thrill, when all Nature seemed to sing a new song, and when your chief delight was to be alone with the Lord, to look into His face, and in silent adoration sit while you listened to His voice? Oh, if that old-time delight has passed, nothing can make up for it to Him or to you.

And now briefly notice the counsel He gives to this church, an injunction, a warning, and a promise. The injunction may be expressed in three words, Remember, Repent, and Repeat. These of course are not the exact words that the Master used, but they will help us to bear in mind the terms of His counsel.

"Remember therefore from whence thou art fallen," go back and think of the freshness of first love. Remind your heart of the light that never was on sea or land when you began to love Him. Go back to the rising life of the Spring-time. "Remember." Oh, the tenderness of that word of Christ. Do not be satisfied any longer with the dead level of your orthodoxy, and your mechanical precision in service. "Remember therefore from whence thou art fallen."

And then "repent." Turn back in heart and purpose of the old attitude, the attitude

The Ephesus Letter

of simplicity and purity, the abandonment of everything for love, the love of espousal, the first love that leaves father and mother and house and lands and everything for the loved one. Go back to that, return and do the first works. And what are the first works? Let Jesus tell us, " This is the work of God, that ye believe on Him Whom He hath sent." Christ said in effect to these people, ' Your lack of love proves your failure of faith. You do not believe in Me as you did, or you would love Me as of old. You have lost confidence. An absolute confidence always blossoms into a perfect love. And if the fruit of your love be smitten, it is because at the root of your faith is some disease.'

Then finally mark His solemn warning. " Or else I come to thee, and will move thy lampstand out of its place, except thou repent." What is this He says? Remove thy lampstand? Yes, notwithstanding all the perfection of your work, and your labour, and your patience, notwithstanding your cold and icy purity, notwithstanding your orthodoxy, unless you love, that lampstand must be removed. It is impossible to witness for Christ in the darkness of the world except in the power of first love. It is not abundant works, nor even a passionate determination to witness against the sin of the world that serves Him. Unless there be first love the lampstand must be removed. It is a solemn warning. Oh, that we might rightly understand it, and see that it is not merely a capricious threatening, but the statement of an inevitable sequence. Loss of first love to Christ will inevitably issue in loss of love to the brethren, and cannot fail to dry up the rivers of compassion toward the outside world. It is the first love of the saint that is the true light that shines in a dark place. When men outside the Church can look at its community and say " see how these people love " then they will be attracted to the Centre upon which our love is set. Without first love we may retain ceaseless activity, immaculate purity, severest orthodoxy, but there will be no light shining in a dark place.

It is not our doing that lightens the world. It is not our ceremonial cleanness that helps men. It is not our correctness in the holding of truth that helps a dying race. It is our love first for our Master, then for each other, and then for the world.

Then notice the graciousness of the closing promise. "To him that overcometh, to him will I give to eat of the tree of life, which is in the Paradise of God." And how may a man overcome? By remembering, repenting, and repeating, by coming back to the beginnings. Then shall he have to eat of the tree of life. See how the great words gather together. Life, light, love. They are the very words that Jesus came to bring us, and it is only as we have life that we love, and only as we love that we shed forth light.

The supreme lesson of this study for to-day is that for the maintenance of our position as light-bearers our communion with the Master in all the abandonment of first love must be maintained. "If I speak with the tongues of men and of angels, but have not love, I am become sounding brass, or a clanging cymbal. And if I have the gift of prophecy, and know all mysteries and all knowledge; and if I have all faith, so as to remove mountains, but have not love, I am nothing. And if I bestow all my goods to feed the poor, and if I give my body to be burned, but have not love, it profiteth me nothing."

THE SMYRNA LETTER

"And to the angel of the church in Smyrna write: "These things saith the first and the last, which was dead, and lived again: I know thy tribulation, and thy poverty (but thou art rich), and the blasphemy of them which say they are Jews, and they are not, but are a synagogue of Satan. Fear not the things which thou art about to suffer: behold, the devil is about to cast some of you into prison, that ye may be tried; and ye shall have tribulation ten days. Be thou faithful unto death, and I will give thee the crown of life. He that hath an ear, let him hear what the Spirit saith to the churches. He that overcometh shall not be hurt of the second death." Rev. ii: 8-11.

IV

THE SMYRNA LETTER

SMYRNA has been for long centuries a prosperous city. Originally an Ionian settlement, it passed for a period into obscurity. It was rebuilt by Alexander the Great and Antigonus, and almost immediately it became noted and wealthy.

We have no account in Scripture of the planting of the church there, but history tells the story of the persecution of the church, and chronicles the fact of the martyrdom of Polycarp in his ninetieth year. History moreover clearly states the cause of the persecution, showing that it arose from the clamour of the pagan population, excited and incensed by the Jewish community. This statement is valuable as throwing much light upon some of the things incidentally referred to in the epistle itself.

The Master addressing the church, speaks of Himself as "The first and the last, which was dead, and lived again." These words are a repetition of those which He had addressed to John when, smitten with a great fear in the presence of His glory, he had become as one dead. This church is in the midst of a great sorrow, and the Lord announces Himself as the living One Who has passed through death, and therefore possesses the keys of death and of Hades. In approaching a people dwelling in the region and shadow of death, some of their number having already suffered martyrdom, others of them most certainly approaching the place of death through their loyalty to Him, He reminds them that He is Master of these darker matters also, and holds in His own hand the keys. The description is intended for the consolation of the afflicted people, and indeed out of this description by which our Lord introduces Himself to their notice, flows all the comfort that follows. They are in the midst of sorrow, and He first declares to them that He has been to the uttermost reach of it, and is alive again. They are under the shadow of death, and He tells them that He " has been dead, and is alive forevermore." They are almost certainly in the midst of those perplexities and questionings which come to men when surrounded by sorrow. He tells them that He, having been dead, is now alive; and, moreover, that He holds the keys of death and of Hades, the symbols of solution and au-

The Smyrna Letter

thority. He has unlocked the problem and is now Master of the situation.

The Master's method in commending this church at Smyrna is remarkable. He offers them no solution of the problem of their pain, and it may be said that the commendation is contained in a silence and a parenthesis. His approval of this church is manifest not so much by what He said, as by the fact that He had no complaint to make concerning them. Added to the silence there is one brief phrase, parenthetically interjected, four words only, "But thou art rich." A careful investigation will show the value of this phrase, and who would not rather have that illuminative flash-light than all the eulogy that fell from His lips on the church at Ephesus? Here as ever, the value of the statement depends upon the fact that it was Christ Who uttered it. We shall only be able to understand the silence of Jesus and this parenthetical commendation by a careful examination of the surroundings. Let us endeavour to see it as He reveals it.

Of it he says, "I know"—three things. "Thy tribulation, and thy poverty, and the blasphemy of them which say they are Jews, and they are not, but are a synagogue of Satan." Let us mention these separately. "I know thy tribulation." "I know thy poverty." "I know the blasphemy of them which say they are Jews and they are not, but are a synagogue of Satan." Tribulation, poverty, reviling. These are the words which reveal the desperate condition of the church at the moment when the Master sent His message to them.

First, "I know thy tribulation." This is a strong word, not very often made use of. It signifies a pressure of persecution. Jesus did not say I know thy trials, the occasional testings of faith, those experiences which are common to all the saints and necessary for their perfecting, but "thy tribulation." Our word tribulation suggests the stripe of the Roman whip, but the word that the Master used, suggested rather the pressure of the stones that grind the wheat, or that force the blood out of the grape. It is a word that throbs with meaning. These people were being pressed even to death on account of their loyalty to Christ, and as He looks at the church, He says in tones of infinite tenderness, "I know thy tribulation."

And yet again, "I know thy poverty." And the word indicates actual beggary. Here it has no reference to a poverty of spirit. In all

The Smyrna Letter 61

probability these people had suffered the loss of all things in the persecution that had broken out against them, loss of trade, loss of social position, loss almost of the bare necessaries of life, reduced to beggary, "I know thy poverty."

And once more, "I know the blasphemy of them which say they are Jews, and they are not, but are a synagogue of Satan." The use of the word blasphemy is somewhat peculiar here. Evidently the Lord uses the word, not in its specific sense as against God, but in its simplest sense, that of vilification or reviling. Here the Master reveals His intimate knowledge of the causes from which all the trouble has proceeded. In all probability the vilifying of the church by the synagogue had issued in the beggary of the little band of Christians by the pagans of Smyrna. The members of the Jewish synagogue, hating the Christian disciples would publish libellous statements concerning them as to their character, their purpose, and their modes of life. The stories told had aroused the pagan population, and in all likelihood, there had followed the confiscation of their goods which had reduced them to the point of actual want. It is profoundly interesting to notice the wonderful similarity existing between the experience of these people at Smyrna, and the experience of the Lord Himself. The consciousness of this seems to lie within the phrase "which is alive again." Before beginning to speak to them, He reminded them of His own experience; and declared to them that He, having passed through it, has found it the gate of life.

That through which they are passing is in many senses almost identical with that through which He has passed. The force which encompassed His death was the blasphemy of the Jews, acting upon a pagan nation, that stripped Him of all He possessed, and gave Him only death. The persecution that culminated in His own passing had begun within the synagogue, at the very centre of supposed religion, and had proceeded along the line of pagan power to its terrible issue.

Thus addressing these people He says "I know," and the force of the word is not merely that He knows by watching, but by His own experience, not alone by observing their suffering, but by having Himself passed through the same experience. I know for I have experienced the pain of vilification, and the want of poverty, and the final tribulation. I know all these to their deepest depths. Thus He

The Smyrna Letter

would comfort them with a declaration of His consciousness of their condition, and His experimental sympathy therewith.

With what summary conciseness and startling force He sums up in a sentence the truth concerning the condition of the Jews in Smyrna. They are "a synagogue of Satan," and these are they that have persecuted His people. Mark the contrast. The church in Smyrna. A synagogue of Satan. The ecclesia of the living God, the gathered out people. A synagogue of Satan, the gathered together forces. It is a terrible indictment, called forth by the fact that they had vilified His people, and so had proved themselves under the leadership of the slanderer whose perpetual aim it is to degrade our God and His Christ.

Thus He identified Himself with them in their sorrow and suffering, and thus in a sentence uttered the most severe condemnation of those who were causing the trouble.

Now let us mark the commendation. First the silence, and what can be said concerning silence. It is more eloquent than all language. He has no word of complaint to utter. The character and conduct of the church at Smyrna was such as perfectly to satisfy the heart of the Lord, and how wonderful it is when we remember that tribulation and poverty and reviling make more terrible demands than any other circumstances, upon the spirit of those passing through it. There is no profounder proof of grace of character than that of being able to suffer wrongfully and yet to manifest a gracious spirit. How often have we all fallen at that very point. Repeatedly in the midst of suffering for righteousness sake, we have manifested unrightness of character and of conduct. Is not that the whole story of the failure of God's wonderful servant Moses. " He spake unadvisedly with his lips." And yet the people were doing wrong. There was no possible defence of their action, but in the presence of their wrong-doing, he did wrong, in that he manifested a provoked spirit. Christ watched these saints at Smyrna, persecuted, beggared, vilified, and yet had no fault to find with them. Their spirit under tribulation was such as to satisfy the heart of Christ. The finer graces of the Christian character are only revealed under bruising and pressure, as the fragrance of fine spices is only obtained through crushing. Christ pre-eminently became a sweet smelling savour to God through the terrible experiences of the Cross. His un-

The Smyrna Letter 65

provoked and tender spirit was most perfectly seen amid the circumstances that were provocative of anger and resentment. So with these loved ones in Smyrna. Though under press and conflict, He found nothing to condemn, and in the silence there lies the highest eulogium.

Of such value is this teaching that I pause to make a passing application. Some child of God, whelmed with great and crushing sorrows is longing for the sound of His voice, and there is nothing but silence. It may be that that silence is a sign, not of disapproval but of approval. Do not be cast down. If in the midst of tribulation and suffering there is no voice, it may be that the silence of the Lord is His highest commendation. There is an old and beautiful story of how a nun dreamed that she saw three other nuns at prayer. As they kneeled the Master approached them. As He came to the first of the three, He bent over her with tender solicitude, and smiles full of radiant love, speaking to her in words of softest tenderest music. Leaving her and approaching the next He only placed His hand upon her head, and gave her one look of tender approval. But the third woman He passed almost abruptly without word or glance. The woman in her dream said to herself, How tenderly the Lord must love this first of His children. The second He is not angry with, and yet for her has no endearments like those bestowed upon the first. She wondered how the third had grieved Him, so that He gave her no look, no passing word. As in her dream she attempted to account for the action of the Lord, the Master Himself confronted her, and addressing her said, " Oh woman of the world, —how wrongly hast thou judged. The first kneeling woman needs all the succour of My constant care to keep her feet in the way. The second has stronger faith and deeper love, but the third whom I seemed to pass abruptly by, has faith and love of finest fibre, and her I am preparing by swift processes for highest and holiest service. She knows and loves and trusts Me so perfectly as to be independent of words or looks."

Do not therefore be surprised if you have no vision. It may be that the vision granted is after all but proof of weakness. Peter, James, and John were taken to behold the vision of transfiguration. The common interpretation of this is that they were special apostles being prepared for special service, and while unable to contradict that, I should not personally be

The Smyrna Letter 67

surprised in the perfect day to discover that the reasons for the Master's special attention were to be found in their weakness rather than their strength. Not a word of commendation did He speak to the church in Smyrna, but a great silence as they passed through the fire proved His approval of the rightness of their spirit.

And yet there was more than the silence, just that one word, that flash, that gleam of light, " but thou art rich." It is as though He bent over them and whispered the great truth. Smyrna counts thee poor. I count thee rich. The blasphemy of the Jews and the persecution of pagans have robbed thee of everything, but thou hast lost nothing. I know the pinch of poverty, I know its pain, and yet I never lost the riches of spiritual wealth. While I was still upon the earth a man, I was a beggar, and yet My Father was with Me. " I know thy poverty (but thou art rich)."

The words recall to our mind, the Lord's conception of riches as revealed in His parable concerning the rich fool. He said to himself, " I will say to my soul, Soul, thou hast much goods laid up for many years." As though a life could be fed with goods! And yet the only place of worship for many is a dry goods store. Dry goods indeed! At the close of the parable Jesus said, "So is he that layeth up treasure for himself, and is not rich toward God." Of goods these Smyrna saints had none, but they were rich toward God. "I know thy poverty," thou hast no barns, no store-house, but thou hast all wealth.

Again one calls to mind the word of James, the practical, far-seeing apostle. "Did not God choose them that are poor as to the world to be rich in faith." This also is what the Master meant. "I know thy poverty," you are poor as to the world. They have taken everything from you, but you are rich in faith, in the principle that possesses the unseen and imperishable things.

And yet again, the words of Paul recur. His conception of his own position perfectly harmonizes with the Lord's estimate of the people in Smyrna. "As poor"—so poor that he had to make tents to live, so poor that when someone is coming to see him, he has to ask them to bring that old cloak to protect him from the cold, and to keep him warm—" yet making many rich "—so rich that he is able to minister through tent-making without cost, so rich that he is more anxious about the parchments than about the cloak,—" especially the

The Smyrna Letter 69

parchments." "As having nothing," he writes, "and yet possessing all things." "I know thy poverty," says Christ, you are poor, you have nothing, but you are rich, enriching others, possessing all things.

All this is intensely interesting, but we have not yet touched the deepest note of exposition. Read again the old familiar words concerning the Master from the writings of Paul. "For ye know the grace of our Lord Jesus Christ, that, though He was rich, yet for your sakes He became poor, that ye through His poverty might become rich." The words used are exactly the same, the same for "rich" and the same for "poverty." "He became poor," "I know thy poverty." "He was rich," "but thou art rich." "I know, *I* know your poverty. I have been poor with the actual poverty of beggary, but you are rich, for through that poverty of Mine, you have entered into that wealth of Mine, and even in the midst of all your poverty, you possess the abiding wealth. I know your poverty, for I have shared it. I know your wealth, for I have given it." It is well to remember that the word "rich" in all these cases is the actual word which we use of the world's wealth. It is the root word from which we derive our word plutocrat. According to Christ then, wealth is enrichment of character, not possession of gold. He said in effect to these suffering people in Smyrna, You are the poorest people in Smyrna. You are the plutocrats of Smyrna. Others have the wealth of the world, the fulness of material things, but you have the true fulness. I love to think of this estimate of Christ, and to remember that the saints of God are the true aristocrats and plutocrats of every age. An aristocrat is a man of best strength. A plutocrat is a full man. The best strength of the nation is ever to be found in the saints of Christ. The true fulness of the nation is to be reckoned by the number of its men and women who are living in fellowship with God. The riches of the saints are the riches that abide. The things the Christians of Smyrna had lost, they must have left behind them ere long, when they had passed from the stage of earthly action. The things that they possessed became theirs in fullest measure only through that passing. True wealth is the wealth that never tarnishes, never decays, never fades. Oh, glorious parenthesis of Jesus, a great silence of commendation, and a parenthesis of approbation.

What words of counsel then has He to speak

The Smyrna Letter

to people passing through such circumstances? Mainly two. First, "Fear not," and secondly, "Be thou faithful unto death." In reading this epistle I think the most startling thing to me was to discover that there is not a single promise to them that they should escape their suffering. Nay, He rather tells them that heavier trials are to come upon them, and the "fear not" is a preparatory word in advance of the present consciousness of need. He does not say "Fear not the things which thou hast suffered," but "Fear not the things which thou art about to suffer." There is no promise of succour. He does not say, Never mind, these things will soon be over. He comes rather with an announcement of another sorrow. Oh, the comfort of knowing that He is acquainted with the things that are yet to be, and that facing them He says " fear not." There is no sorrow waiting for them that He is not acquainted with. I know thy present tribulation. I know thy present poverty, the present blasphemy I know. I know more. I know what lies hidden in the womb of the future, that "the devil is about to cast some of you into prison, that ye may be tried, and ye shall have tribulation ten days." Fear not these things then, the persecution will increase, the fearsome darkness will deepen, tribulation will be more severe, the pressure will yet be heavier. Fear not, and let the first comforting thought against fear be that I know and that I have told you.

Then "Be thou faithful unto death," live upon the principle of faith even to the bound of death. The word "faithful" here is from the root which means to be convinced. Fidelity is born of conviction, and conviction must have a groundwork and foundation. What then is this faithfulness enjoined? The faithfulness of the saints is the assurance of the faithfulness of Jesus. A deep conviction of His fidelity produces their fidelity. Wherever a man, woman, or child under any circumstances of pain or testing is deeply convinced of the fidelity of Christ, they are immediately and necessarily faithful themselves. It is as though He had said to them, You are going to be cast into prison, "the devil is about to cast some of you into prison, that ye may be tried." Be faithful, believe still. Live within the limit of a great assurance. Don't question Me, don't doubt Me, depend on Me. The Lord did not mean, Gather yourselves up and go through. He simply meant, Trust Me. He did not intend to advise them to gird up their loins and be determined that they would see the business through. That is ever a poor and sorry way of attempting to pass through times of testing. He meant rather, Trust Me, let Me be your courage. I am alive, and I was dead. I have gone to the limit of this matter. There is no depth I have not fathomed, no darkness I have not penetrated. Be faithful, follow Me, not in the effort of a strenuous determination, but with the ease of a simple trust.

Then the gracious promise. "I will give thee the crown of life," and the word is very full and very rich. This crown that He promises is the crown of royalty. It is more. It is the crown of royalty victorious. It is still more. It is the chaplet that adorns the brow of the victor who comes laden with spoils, the crown of royalty, the crown of victory, the crown of added wealth. It is the crown of life, life which reigns because it has won, and reigns moreover in possession of spoils obtained through conflict. The life is the crown. What wondrous light this flings back upon the process. This pressure of tribulation is not accidental and capricious. Out of the tribulation we shall have our triumph. Out of the darkness we shall come to light. That is the whole philosophy of suffering.

This may be a message to some saints who are being sorely tried. And yet are you not already, as the mists clear from the valleys, finding your crown of life? I think to-day I see the meaning of past mysteries in my own life. Out of the pressure of tribulation we extract the new wine of the Kingdom, and out of the deep dark death experience in which the devil sifts and tries, there breaks a new capacity, an enlarged outlook, a new meaning in life, a new tone in the speech. Almost imperceptibly and yet surely, through the process of pain God is putting the horizon further back, and broadening and deepening the experience of life. That is the present value of pain, but its ultimate value is the fulness of which all this is but the foretelling. When presently all the tribulation is passed, and the painful processes of the little while are over, and the last grim pressure ceases, then we shall be crowned with life, then we shall know the meaning of life.

All this must ever be emphasized by the perpetual memory of the words with which Christ addressed His suffering saints. Emphasizing His experimental acquaintance with the philosophies, He declares " I was dead, and behold, I am alive." " I know thy tribula-

The Smyrna Letter 75

tion!" Think of His tribulation. "I know thy poverty!" Think of His poverty. "I know the revilings of them which say they are Jews and they are not!" Think of the revilings heaped upon Him by them which said they were Jews. "Fear not!" Think of His unswerving faith in God. "Be thou faithful until death!" See Him faithful unto death. "I will give thee the crown of life!" See Him crowned with life, on the resurrection morning. This is the heart and centre of the great truth delivered to the suffering saints at Smyrna. I am your companion in distress. I am your comrade in the darkness. I know, and I am with you, and just beyond I will be with you still, leading you to the fountains of living waters.

Then there was His added promise. "He that overcometh shall not be hurt of the second death." It always seems to me as though this were an inferential note of warning and threatening against the persecutors. These men of Smyrna will die, saints and sinners alike, but beyond death is death. The persecutors of Smyrna will pass through death to death. The believers of Smyrna being faithful to death, through death will find no second death, but instead thereof life. The saints are rich in poverty. They walk through darkness into light.

They live beyond all death. As Christ holds the keys, we see through open doors, things as they really are. The great and wealthy men of Smyrna were not the persecuting pagans and the blasphemous Jews, but the suffering, tried, poverty-stricken saints, for they were wealthy in all essential things, and would pass through the pressure of death to the realization of endless life.

Let all Smyrna face death, but only those whose principle of life is faith in Christ will pass unafraid through the first to find the second abolished.

Of this epistle there can be no immediate application to the majority of those who hear these words. Sometimes it seems as though the very reproach of Christ has almost ceased. I am not sure that this is a healthy sign. It is doubtful if many people really suffer much to-day for Christ's sake. I often hear men speak of the difficulties of their position in business, of the taunts and sneers of certain opposing ones, but are they really serious when they mention these things? When we think of the actualities of the persecution in Smyrna, and of the early days of the Christian era, ought we not to blush to speak of suffering to-day? And yet is there not a sadness in this

The Smyrna Letter 77

very fact of absence of persecution? Is real Godliness more popular to-day, or is not that which is popular a kind of hybrid Christianity? I leave these questions for personal asking.

And yet there is a sympathetic application of the epistle. During the Armenian massacres, and the martyrdom of native Christians in China, how one has thanked God again and again for the letter to Smyrna. Surely the One walking amid the lampstands said to all these, as robbed of earthly possessions, and brutally deprived of life they were still faithful to His name, " I know . . . but thou art rich." I think I hear the voice of the thorn-crowned sounding in cadences of sweetest music over the hills and valleys of Armenia, and I think I hear that self-same voice, like the voice of many waters, breathing these words of strength to all His witnesses in China. Surely He met them at the portal of death, and crowned them with life.

And yet there is an immediate application to all those who suffer for His name's sake.

From the meditation, let us gather one or two lessons of general import. First, outward adversity of a church or a people or a person is not a proof of essential poverty or weakness. It is not always the wealthy church financially

78 A First Century Message

that is the rich church. The material wealth of members does not create the true riches of the church. How often it has been that some struggling company of believers, fighting with poverty, contending for very existence, has been the truly rich and prosperous church.

Then secondly, let us gather the inexpressible comfort that comes from this revelation of Christ's identification with all His suffering saints. Wherever the Church passes through tribulation, He stands and says "I know."

And lastly, let us ever rejoice in His assertion that He holds the keys of all the things that most affright and oppress us, of the last foes, of death and of Hades, and the keys in His right hand are symbols of solution and authority. As we pass to the valley of the shadow, He approaches, holding these keys, and saying, "Fear not," I have unlocked the problem. I have solved it, I have been into the deepest darkness, I know it. I have not borrowed these keys. They belong to Me. I have them for unlocking and for locking.

Oh, suffering saints, and all who approach the shadow-land, fear not, fear not! Trust Him utterly, be faithful, confiding, even unto death, and through the dark chambers of death and of Hades, He will lead to light. Christ never tells us not to fear, until He Himself has fathomed all the mystery. I say to my child Do not be afraid, while yet in my own heart lurks a great fear that I dare not tell him of. This Christ never does. He has not fear, and therefore I need not fear but may sing with the Psalmist,

" Yea, though I walk through the valley of the shadow of death,
I will fear no evil; for Thou art with me:
Thy rod and Thy staff, they comfort me."

He has probed the shadow and the pain. Let Him lead on, even through tribulation and through death, to the life and the crowning that lie ahead.

THE PERGAMUM LETTER

"And to the angel of the church in Pergamum write;

"These things saith He that hath the sharp two-edged sword: I know where thou dwellest, even where Satan's throne is: and thou holdest fast My name, and didst not deny My faith, even in the days of Antipas My witness, My faithful one, who was killed among you, where Satan dwelleth. But I have a few things against thee, because thou hast there some that hold the teaching of Balaam, who taught Balak to cast a stumblingblock before the children of Israel, to eat things sacrificed to idols, and to commit fornication. So hast thou also some that hold the teaching of the Nicolaitans in like manner. Repent therefore; or else I come to thee quickly, and I will make war against them with the sword of My mouth. He that hath an ear, let him hear what the Spirit saith to the churches. To him that overcometh, to him will I give of the hidden manna, and I will give him a white stone, and upon the stone a new name written, which no one knoweth but he that receiveth it." Rev. ii: 12-17.

V

THE PERGAMUM LETTER

PERGAMUM was an illustrious city of Mysia, given over almost entirely to wealth and fashion. Unlike Ephesus and Smyrna, it was not a centre of commerce. Æsculapius, the god of medicine, was worshipped there under the form of a serpent, and the special aspect of this worship was that of the study of the secret springs of life, and like all Nature worship, sincere as may have been the beginnings thereof, it had issued in corruption. This fact may serve to throw light upon some of the statements that occur in the letter.

We have no account whatever of the planting of the church, and therefore can only look at it as seen in the epistle now under consideration.

Christ speaks to the church as the One "that hath the sharp two-edged sword." That sword as we have seen is the symbol of the discerning and executive power of truth. The fitness of this lies in the fact that the church is harbouring error. Not that the church has itself adopted the teaching, nor that she has as a corporate whole, committed herself to these heresies, but she has become guilty of Broad Churchism, attempting to find room within her pale for all sorts and conditions of men and faiths.

Approaching the church as the One from Whose mouth proceeds the sword, He comes to deal with the false teachers within it.

First let us notice His commendation. " I know where thou dwellest, even where Satan's throne is: and thou holdest fast My name, and didst not deny My faith, even in the days of Antipas My witness, My faithful one, who was killed among you, where Satan dwelleth." The Lord recognizes the peculiar dangers and difficulties surrounding these people. The underlying suggestion of the commendation is that it is an honourable thing to have held fast His name, and not have denied His faith. The inference is that if there was any place that it might have been probable that people should have ceased to hold His name, it would have been in these peculiar and difficult circumstances in which the church at Pergamum found itself at the time.

The commendation consists in the twofold statement. "Thou holdest fast My name,"

The Pergamum Letter

"Thou didst not deny My faith." "My name, My faith." And the emphasis of the commendation is discovered by consideration of the peculiar perils threatening these people. "I know where thou dwellest." That statement in itself is full of comfort. In every circumstance of trial and tribulation and persecution and peril, we may hear the words of the Master, "I know where thou dwellest."

In this case the place is described by the startling phrase, "Where Satan's throne is." Satan has ever some base of operation, some central place for his throne. It is very difficult to refer to Satan without wanting to say a great deal about him, and much needs to be said in these days; and in a study of this epistle it is necessary to pause for a little upon this subject. Wasting no time over arguments concerning the personality of Satan, but accepting that as an established fact, there remains certain co-related facts which need restatement. First, Satan is not God, and therefore neither has he any of the essential powers of Deity. He is neither omniscient, omnipresent, nor omnipotent. He does not know as God knows. He is not everywhere as God is everywhere. He is not all-powerful as God is all-powerful. He is a fallen angel, "Lucifer, son of the morning, how art thou fallen." In his fall and degradation, he has retained all the essential capacities of his unfallen state. The wisdom, the possibility of locomotion, and the marvellous power, which were his before he fell, are his to-day, but he is not God. He dragged with him in that awful fall hosts of the bright ones, and with the marvellous wisdom of that unfallen nature, now prostituted to base uses, he marshalls them for the doing of his work. To state the case bluntly, if the devil is here, he is not there. If the devil is there he is not here. His messengers cover all countries, and include all ranks of life in their operations, and these ramifications of evil are under the supreme control of Satan, who is the prince of the power of the air, the god of this world, the son of the morning, fallen as lightning from heaven. For the carrying out of his enterprises in the world, he has somewhere a place where his throne is, a base of operations. It may be that he has more than one such centre, and he himself will pass from point to point with the rapidity of lightning. He is ubiquitous, as we use the word of a general who, on the field of battle seems to be here, there, and everywhere, only more so. He is not omnipresent as God is without motion

The Pergamum Letter

and without effort. At the time of the writing of this letter, for some strategic reason of his own, he had his seat at Pergamum. The Master knew it and indicated it. Truly the devil manifests a great deal more wisdom than Christian people very often. His throne will be at some strategic point from which he can best use his influence. Almost invariably that throne is at the centre of worldliness and worldly greatness. Wherever his throne is, is a place of peculiar peril. As it has been forcefully said, " In the greatest centres of worldly power, there his eye more peculiarly watches, his energy more peculiarly acts, his influence more peculiarly emanates."

Now this was the peril of the church at Pergamum. In Smyrna it was " a synagogue of Satan." In Pergamum it is the " throne of Satan." In Smyrna opposition to the Christian Church was veiled behind religion. The devil operated through the Jewish synagogue, and Christ with infinite scorn and contempt, spoke of that religious centre as the " synagogue of Satan." In Pergamum it is quite a different matter. Satan's throne is there, and the peril that threatens the church is not so much that of direct opposition as that of patronage. " Where Satan's throne is," the saints are in peril of entering into alliance with the forces under his control.

The history of evil I think will prove the assertion that Satan loves to have his seat in the midst of worldly wealth, and all that stands for the feeding of the flesh life in men. The Master did not say to men what we often say, "Ye cannot serve God and the devil." I do not question the accuracy of that statement, but it is worthy of notice that the Master said, "Ye cannot serve God and Mammon." Thus He revealed the antithesis between the two great forces which govern human lives, God and Mammon. God governs man through the spiritual side of man's nature, and man can only be governed in the highest aspects of his life when he is so governed. Mammon, which stands for all the worldly power and worldly greatness, the things which the men of the world value, as a governing force issues in the degradation of man, proving he cannot be perfectly governed in flesh by the things that minister to flesh. The devil lurks behind Mammon, sets his throne up at the point where it gathers its force, and from there rules men. If you think to-day for a single moment of the great evils that are blighting our lands, and if you take time to think far enough back in the history of these things, you will discover that the invariable impulse of evil is Mammon, and the love of gold. Behind the drink traffic, behind the unholy and iniquitous crowding of the poor into dwellings of which our cities ought to be ashamed, behind the breath of vile impurity that spoils life as it passes across it, is Mammon, the love of gold; and behind that, using and manipulating it, the devil sits upon the throne of power.

The peril which ever threatens a church situated in such a city is that it may enter into alliance with Mammon, and so pass under the control of Satan. Pergamum was perhaps the wealthiest city of the seven, and there was Satan's throne, the base of his operations, the place from which he governed the goings of evil in that whole district. If you ask me where Satan's throne is in England, I do not hesitate to say that it is in London. If you ask me where his throne is in America, it would be difficult to answer, for there seem to be several places, one in the East at least, one in the middle West, a strategic point, and others there may be on the far West coast, where the gates are opening towards yet further enterprises. Be sure of this that where the excellencies of God's earth create special possibilities for man's abuse, there the devil sets his throne.

Having recognized this peril, let us now notice the commendation. "Thou holdest fast My name." Christ's name is ever the symbol of His nature, and this first word of commendation declares that the church at Pergamum has been loyal to the Person of Christ. There had been no denying of any part of the strange and mystic fact of His personality, that personality that can be compared to nothing, and that can have nothing compared to it. His name stands for a Person utterly separated from all others, and utterly unlike them in its totality, while akin to God and man in its duality. Christ says You have not denied My name. You are loyal to the central fact of Christianity. Thou holdest fast My name, which is the sign and symbol of My nature.

Again, "Thou didst not deny My faith." Note specially that He does not say, You have not denied your own faith, but "My faith." In the letter to the Hebrews the writer speaks of Jesus as being the "Author and Finisher," not of our faith, but "of faith." That is to say, He lived and wrought upon the principle of faith, and through His victory, was the Author or the File-leader, as the word literally

The Pergamum Letter 91

is, and Perfector, or Vindicator of faith as a principle of life. The faith of man exercised in His victory, is response to His faith. The fact that the church at Pergamum had not denied the faith, indicates that they were loyal, not only to the Person of Christ, but that they evidently rested in His accomplished purpose. His faith had operated to perfect realization of a Divine purpose of redemption. Their faith operated in Him for the appropriation of that redemption. The redemption was that of regeneration as justification, renewal as sanctification, realization as glorification. The force that was sufficient to bring Him to victory was that of His faith in God and His faith in men, faith, that is, in the wisdom and the love of God, and in the possibility of man brought under the influence of that wisdom and that love. This was the mighty principle that bore Him up and carried Him on, until His faith, triumphant even over death, became the life principle for ruined men, and their faith centred upon His victory, appropriated the value of His faith. His faith would have been denied by their lack of faith in Him. On the other hand, His faith is affirmed by that confidence in Him which created their character, and issued in conduct. " Thou holdest fast My name" is the commendation of Christ upon the loyalty of the men of Pergamum to His Person; the peculiar, separate, unique Person of Jesus Christ, the one and only Person of His order that the world has ever seen. The name of Jesus stands for His personality, for the human and the Divine, for the Divine and the human, for that strange mysterious combination that has baffled the theology of every successive century, and concerning which no final word has yet been said because no final word can ever be said, because no finite mind can grasp the infinite mystery of God incarnate. To that name these men had held fast.

"Thou didst not deny My faith," indicates their confidence in His mission, confidence in His atoning work. His name marks the glory of His Person. His faith marks the perfection of His purpose. It was a wonderful testimony that the Master bore to this church at Pergamum, where Satan's throne was, the centre of wealth and power, the home of mystic thought and occult study. The church had been loyal to the Person of Christ, more mysterious than the mysteries of Pergamum, loyal to the faith of Christ, bringing men to the true springs of life, which these dwellers in the wealthy city

The Pergamum Letter

were professing to give themselves over to discover.

Now mark His complaint. "But I have a few things against thee, because thou hast there some that hold the teaching of Balaam, who taught Balak to cast a stumblingblock before the children of Israel, to eat things sacrificed to idols, and to commit fornication." That is one thing. "So hast thou also some that hold the teaching of the Nicolaitans in like manner." That is the second thing. Let us examine them for they reveal one great fact to which the Lord objects in this church at Pergamum. It is necessary that we note carefully what is here said. A very tender and delicate distinction is drawn between the church and certain persons within the church. He has something against the church, but He is careful to show that it is not that the church holds the false doctrine, but that she has fellowship with those who do. Not "I have a few things against thee, because thou holdest the teaching of Balaam," but "I have a few things against thee, because thou hast there some that hold the teaching of Balaam." The church was loyal to the mission of Christ, and did not deny the faith, but what He had against them was that they were tolerating false views. What the church lacked was discipline. What cursed the church was a false charity. For the emphasis of this point notice the closing words of the Master, "Repent therefore; or else I come to *thee* quickly, and I will make war against *them* with the sword of My mouth." With great delicacy and fine distinction He draws the line between the church and those holding the false doctrine, and yet He now declares it as being against the whole church, that it tolerates these people within its borders.

What then is the doctrine which is being tolerated and to which our Lord takes objection? "Some that hold the teaching of Balaam, who taught Balak to cast a stumblingblock before the children of Israel, to eat things sacrificed to idols, and to commit fornication." What is this teaching of Balaam? Let us look very carefully at the structure of the statement. "I have a few things against thee, because thou hast there some that hold the teaching of Balaam "—and then there really follows a parenthesis—" who taught Balak to cast a stumblingblock before the children of Israel." Omit the parenthesis, and then read the statement. "I have a few things against thee, be-

The Pergamum Letter

cause thou hast there some that hold the teaching of Balaam, to eat things sacrificed to idols, and to commit fornication."

Now is it to be understood that the Master meant that Balaam's teaching was that men were to eat things sacrificed to idols, and to commit fornication? I think not, although they are the exact things which logically followed the teaching of Balaam, and exactly the same perils which threatened the church at Pergamum.

May we not reverently attempt to paraphrase the words of Christ, so that their meaning may be clearer to us? It is as though He had said, This is what I have against thee. You have people, who in order that they may eat of the things sacrificed to idols, and in order that they may indulge in the sin of fornication, are holding a doctrine which excuses the actual wrong. The wrong thing is the sacrificing to idols and the fornication, but behind the wrong conduct is the wrong creed, and they are holding the doctrine of Balaam in order to excuse or justify conduct which is wrong.

If this be the interpretation then it remains that we should ask, What was the teaching of Balaam, which made possible such awful conduct? The story of Balaam is contained in the book of Numbers, chapters twenty-two to twenty-four, and at the end of the twenty-fourth chapter it would appear as though that story is concluded, but it is not. Let me in few words epitomize the whole story.

Balak, the king of Moab, a man under the influence of the sophistries and incantations of a certain class of men, sent for Balaam. He wanted Balaam to curse the nation that had come up out of Egypt, believing that a curse pronounced would work ruin upon Israel. We do not know who Balaam was. When Balak sent for him, it was that he might hire him. That word "hire" must be carefully remembered in the study. He offered him reward if he would curse Israel.

Now what happened? God appeared to Balaam and warned him not to go. Balak sent his princes back to Balaam, offering him silver and gold and honours if he would but come. Balaam, lured by the hire, started, and on his way encountered that remarkable incident of the appearance of the angel, and the speech of the dumb ass. The result of Balaam's conversation with the angel was that the angel warned him not to go. Balaam terrified, offered to go back, but now the angel said You must go forward. He came to Balak, and on a high mountain seven sacrifices were offered, and he opened his mouth to curse, and instead spoke words of blessing. Balak took him to yet another mountain, with a like result. He hoped that a third place might bring the desired cursing and again the sevenfold sacrifice was offered, and Balaam spoke. There are however, no prophecies in the whole book of God more wonderfully beautiful than the things that then fell from his lips.

The anger of Balak was naturally then kindled, and he said I called you to curse, and behold, thou hast altogether blessed them these three times. He rid himself of Balaam, who returned home. So ends the twenty-fourth chapter.

What then is the doctrine of Balaam? Now the fact is that it has not appeared at all in the story as contained in these chapters. To discover it we must pass into chapter twenty-five, and there we read these startling words, " And Israel abode in Shittim, and the people began to commit whoredom with the daughters of Moab "—that is, with the daughters of this king Balak, and his people. Now specially notice, " *for they* "—that is the children of Moab, and the daughters of Moab, " *called the people unto the sacrifices of their gods; and the people did eat, and bowed down to their gods. And Israel joined himself unto Baal-peor; and the anger of the Lord was kindled against Israel."* Now this is the strangest thing possible. Balaam, instead of cursing the people had blessed them, and the next thing we read is that these very people Moab wanted to destroy, are enticed to the lewd feasts of Moab, and to all the awful corruption that follows upon such a proceeding.

How has this come about? The answer is to be found by passing still further to the thirty-third chapter, of the book of Numbers, and the sixteenth verse, and in the words therein contained, the whole mystery is solved. Moses is speaking, and he says, *" Behold, these,"* that is, the women of Moab, *" caused the children of Israel, through the counsel of Balaam, to commit trespass against the Lord, in the matter of Peor."* Here we touch the secret of the whole thing, and it is a startling revelation. It is evident that when Balaam utterly failed to curse, he went home with the lust of hire still in his heart, and began to corrupt Israel. This he did by persuading them to social alliances with Moab, saying that according to the prophecy he had been forced to utter, Moab would be unable to harm them.

The Pergamum Letter

The doctrine of Balaam broadly stated was undoubtedly that seeing that they were the covenant people of God, they might with safety indulge themselves in social intercourse with their neighbours, for no harm could happen to them. Both Peter and Jude refer to Balaam, and they both tell us that the motive of his teaching was that of hire, but neither of them declare what the teaching was. There can be no reasonable doubt that in effect his declaration to the children of Israel was that their covenant with God was so sure, as would witness the blessing he had been compelled to pronounce, that they need not be anxious about their conduct.

His teaching issued, as Jesus says, in the eating of things sacrificed to idols, and the committing of fornication. It was the perilous and damnable heresy that sin cannot violate a covenant.

Then a second fact in the complaint, "So hast thou also some that hold the teaching of the Nicolaitans in like manner." What that doctrine was I do not profess to know, but I know its issue, and I am not sure that the words "in like manner," do not refer to the similarity between the teaching of the Nicolaitans, and that of Balaam, rather than to the fact that men held that doctrine, as well as the other. Technically there may have been a difference. The issue of both was the same.

What then was the danger in the church at Pergamum? There were persons associated with the church, who held a doctrine which gave them license to indulge in sins which were the special peril of all life in Pergamum. There was the splendour of a great temple worship, with its seductive feasts, and impure gaieties. This question of things sacrificed to idols, and of fornication had arisen long before, and had been remitted to a special council of the church at Jerusalem. The story of that council is recorded in the Acts, chapter fifteen. Its decision was that while they did not desire to insist upon the rite of circumcision, they charged the Christians dwelling in these Asiatic cities that they should not eat things sacrificed to idols, nor commit fornication. In the first letter to the Corinthians, beginning with the sixth chapter, the apostle deals with this very subject of fornication, and of things sacrificed to idols, and he distinctly forbids them on apostolic authority, not merely to the one church at Corinth, but to all the churches of the district, for note well these words, "And so ordain I in all the churches." Thus that

The Pergamum Letter

church had the definite teaching of the apostle that it was wrong to eat the things sacrificed to idols, and yet it was tolerating persons who were finding a way to excuse these popular sins of the city. They held fast the name, they did not deny the faith, but they put false emphasis upon the value of the name, and false application of the force of the faith, claiming that these things were of such value and such force as to cover and make of no vital importance certain forms of popular wrong doing. Thus there was heresy in that church at Pergamum, the heresy which has come to be known in later days as the Antinomian heresy, the heresy which says, You are so safe in the name and in the faith, that it matters little about your conduct. You may mix with the sinners of Pergamum, and follow their habits, and yet share the benefits of the covenant. This is the teaching of Balaam, and it had its recrudescence in the church at Pergamum.

The Lord is terribly severe in His denunciation. The church at Pergamum in its corporate capacity had not indulged in these forbidden sins, neither endorsed the teaching of Balaam. Its fault lay in its lack of discipline, in that it tolerated within its borders those holding the doctrine. The whole church did not hold the doctrine, but for some mistaken idea of expediency and policy, these people were permitting those who did hold it, to remain in fellowship. Said Christ, Thou hast them there. Thou art tolerating the people who hold the doctrine, which can only issue in moral corruption.

Turn now to the counsel. "Repent." This word is addressed not to the people holding the doctrine, but to the church and to the angel. In what sense then can they repent? The only repentance possible to the church was that of the exclusion from its fellowship of the persons who held the pernicious teaching. That doctrine must not be tolerated. The warning is very solemn. "I will make war against them with the sword of My mouth." Unless you exercise your discipline as a church, and exclude these people, I will come and fight against them.

What an inference of love lies behind this threat. It is as though the Lord would say, 'Discipline these people, for the judgment will be swift and heavy, if they are not excluded.' For the sake of the men that hold pernicious doctrine, they should be excluded from the church. There are men in the borders of our churches to whom we are doing incalculable harm by allowing them to remain there. We allow them to remain and they imagine that they are in a place of safety, when they are in the place of death. We are sometimes inclined to treat this warning as though it were not alarming, but I want to say that it is one of the most solemn in all these epistles. It is a warning that the Lord Jesus will come, and by exercise of righteous judgment, will remove what the church itself refuses to remove. The supreme illustration of the solemnity of it is to be found in the letter to the church at Corinth, where disorders had arisen, and Paul wrote words that must have made men tremble before them as to what should be done with the wrongdoers. In that same epistle you will find that the apostle marks this solemn fact, that Jesus Christ, in dealing in judgment with a church, has before now had to remove by death the wrong-doers for the purification of the church, and for the making possible for its testimony of light in the midst of the darkness of the age. If therefore I understand this message of the letter to the church at Pergamum, it is as though the Lord had said, Unless you repent and deal in discipline with these men, I must fight against them with the sword of My mouth, and that sword will not be found to be the method of argument, or a new enunciation of truth. It will be a judgment swift and sure upon the evil workers, in order that the church itself may be free and may be pure.

Then the Lord, in Whose heart there was a great tenderness even toward the evil doers, utters His promise. "To him that overcometh, to him will I give of the hidden manna." That is the first half of the promise, Divine sustenance. And why did Jesus speak of it as manna? Because manna was Divinely supplied, and yet had to be humanly gathered. Hidden manna, the Word of God upon which man lives, as against the doctrine of Balaam, in accepting which man perishes. The true bread, the bread of life. The applicability of this promise to these people is seen when it is remembered how the very heart of the false religion of Pergamum consisted in the attempt to feed upon secret mysteries of life. To those who overcome these subtle temptations, the Master promises that they shall feed upon hidden manna.

And then the other portion of that sweet promise. "To him that overcometh . . . I will give him a white stone, and upon the stone a new name written, which no one knoweth but he that receiveth it." The suggestiveness of that white stone is not perfectly clear. There have been many interpretations. Personally I would be inclined to think that they all have some value. From them let me select four.

The white stone was given to a man who after trial was justly acquitted, and went forth clear from condemnation. The white stone was given to one who, returning from battle, having won victories, bore his triumphs with him. It was the reward of victory. The white stone was sometimes given to a man as the token that he was made a free man of the city. It indicated his free citizenship.

And yet there is one other meaning, perhaps more beautiful than all, very sweet and tender. There was the white stone known as the tessara hospitalis. Two men, friends, about to part, would divide a white stone into two, each carrying with him half, upon which was inscribed the name of the friend. It may be that they would never meet again, but that stone in each case would be bequeathed to son, and sometimes generations after, a man would meet another, and they would find that they possessed the complementary halves of one white stone, and their friendship would be at once created upon the basis of the friendship made long ago.

All these seem to me to be probably suggested by this white stone. First, the white stone of acquittal, which is justification. The white stone of victory, being triumph over all foes. The white stone of citizenship, which marks the freedom of the city of God. And then the white stone of unending friendship, my name written on His half, His name written on mine.

The central lesson of the study is a very solemn one. The Church of Jesus Christ must not tolerate within her borders those who lower the standard of truth's requirements. This is not a question of holding the truth. The church at Pergamum was orthodox. It is a question of the right application of truth. The error of these men is one that in subtle form, threatens all churches even until this hour. It is that if a man's creed be right, his conduct does not so much matter. Truth never excuses sin. All forms of sin are to be treated with ruthless and pitiless severity, and if a man holding any form of teaching, should attempt to excuse sin, he is to be excluded from the fellowship of the saints. Purity of doctrine has its danger. A man may be so loyal to the name and the faith, that almost before he knows it, his zeal for these things may make him blind to the presence of teaching which will undermine their value. The test of doctrine is purity of conduct and character. The seal of the Master has two sides, on each an inscription. On the one side the words are graven, "The Lord knoweth them that are His." On the other side these other words, "Let him that nameth the name of the Lord depart from iniquity." Any attempt to efface this second side of the seal, is blasphemy, an error to be banished with exclusion from the fellowship of the Church. God's order is the order of peace, but it is always peace based upon purity, for the wisdom that is from above is first pure and then peaceable.

THE THYATIRA LETTER

"And to the angel of the church in Thyatira write;

" These things saith the Son of God, Who hath His eyes like a flame of fire, and His feet are like unto burnished brass. I know thy works, and thy love and faith and ministry and patience, and that thy last works are more than the first. But I have against thee, that thou sufferest the woman Jezebel, which calleth herself a prophetess; and she teacheth and seduceth My servants to commit fornication, and to eat things sacrificed to idols. And I gave her time that she should repent; and she willeth not to repent of her fornication. Behold, I do cast her into a bed, and them that commit adultery with her into great tribulation, except they repent of her works. And I will kill her children with death; and all the churches shall know that I am He which searcheth the reins and hearts: and I will give unto each one of you according to your works. But to you I say, to the rest that are in Thyatira, as many as have not this teaching, which know not the deep things of Satan, as they say; I cast upon you none other burden. Howbeit that which ye have, hold fast till I come. And he that overcometh, and he that keepeth My works unto the end, to him will I give authority over the nations: and he shall rule them with a rod of iron, as the vessels of the potter are broken to shivers; as I also have received of My Father: and I will give him the morning star. He that hath an ear, let him hear what the Spirit saith to the churches." Rev. ii: 18-29.

VI

THE THYATIRA LETTER

THYATIRA was a small city in Asia Minor. While we have no certain account of the planting there of the Christian Church, it may be it was an indirect result of the influence of Lydia. We remember how she, the "seller of purple of the city of Thyatira," was one at the prayer meeting held on the banks of the river. There her heart was opened to receive the truth and obey it, and she and all her household were baptized and received into the fellowship of the Church. They belonged to Thyatira, though at the time they were living near Philippi. This of course is pure conjecture. Nothing has been definitely revealed, therefore again we are confined for our knowledge of the church to what appears of it in this letter of Jesus.

In addressing the angel, the Lord announces Himself as the "Son of God, Who hath His eyes like a flame of fire, and His feet are like unto burnished brass." "The Son of God." This is the first time that He has made use of this description of Himself in these letters, and it marks the assertion of power and authority. He is the infallible One to Whose speech the church must pay attention. When John turned to see the vision, he "beheld One like unto a Son of man," but yet the glory of the vision spoke also of the fact that He was Son of God. And now in this central letter of the seven, He makes use of the title of supreme authority. From the complete vision He selects two facts concerning Himself, which indicate the special meaning and value of the message He is about to deliver, "His eyes like a flame of fire, and His feet are like unto burnished brass," the eyes of fire suggesting His intimate knowledge, His penetrating vision concerning the church, so that in the sentence He is about to pronounce, there can be no mistake, for His understanding of all the conditions is a perfect understanding. The eyes of fire pierce all the deeps of darkness, and know the profoundest secrets. He is also the One Who "hath His feet like unto burnished brass," and by these statements He practically announces the fact that He is coming in judgment which is strong and pure. His eyes like a flame of fire, He sees perfectly and understands accurately. His feet like unto burnished brass, He marches to judgment, the King amid the seven golden lampstands, and the track of His coming is the track of fire. Righteous, pure, and final are all His judgments. Within the church at Thyatira there is an evil for which no remedial measures are sufficient. It is not one that admits of correction. There is nothing for it but destruction. It has permeated the whole fellowship. Nothing but judgment remains, and so He comes to definite and immediate dealing with this evil.

His commendation commences with the usual words, "I know." The general statement is "I know thy works." Then follows an analysis, "and thy love and faith and ministry and patience." And lastly, "thy last works are more than the first." Three things are indicated in this commendation. First, the works of the church; secondly, the forces that lie behind the works—"thy love and faith and ministry and patience;" and lastly that those works have not decreased but increased. He thus approves the activity of the church, the principles upon which it is based, and the fact that in true order, it increases. His first approbation is of the church's work, the things that are seen. His second of the hidden facts that lie behind the outward manifestation. Thirdly, He approves that which is always a sequence of such condition, that the last works are more than the first.

"I know thy works." He does not name or tabulate them. He declares His acquaintance with them.

Also He recognizes that behind them lie the love and fidelity, the ministry and the patience, and the fact that because these works have these principles behind them, the last works are more than the first.

Notice principally, though briefly, the principles He recognizes as lying behind the works of the church. "I know . . . thy love." This is a statement of the church's character. It is the fact that lies at the root, and out of which all springs. Underlying all the works there was a principle toward God and man which the Master had declared to be the sum and substance of the law of God. It was a church character. There was no breach, no division, no schism, but a wonderful manifestation of love.

"I know . . . thy faith." Again the force of the word is thy fidelity. Faith is here mentioned not as the principle out of which an attitude grows, but rather the attitude of fidelity that grows out of the principle of confidence. I know thy stedfastness, I know

The Thyatira Letter

that in thee is manifested the opposite of fickleness. Too often works of love are alike occasional and spasmodic, but here they were characterized by constancy. In this case the love was not an accident, it was a habit.

"I know . . . thy ministry," and herein is a tender and beautiful touch. He was conscious of love in action, of deeds done because of love to God and man. There is a difference between this ministry and the general works already referred to. They are the peculiar and special activities of the church of Jesus Christ in its church capacity. The ministry referred to here is rather that of unofficial kindnesses and tendernesses of the members as amongst themselves, and in all probability toward the outsider also. It is possible to have a church characterized by works, and yet sadly devoid of this particular kind of ministry. There have been officials constantly zealous concerning all official work, and yet lacking the thousand tender touches which fulfil this highest ministry. So many men are ready to spread a banquet, and slow to give a cup of cold water. But to this church the Master says, "I know . . . thy ministry, as well as thy works," all the outpouring of the life in untabulated service.

"I know . . . thy patience." This is a great word upon which the Master seemed to set much value. He spoke of it to the church at Ephesus, and now again to this church at Thyatira. May we not define this patience as the spirit of peace under pressure. Surely Milton's words may be taken as a perfect exposition of true patience.

> "Yet I argue not against Heaven's hand or will.
> Nor bate a jot of heart or hope,
> But still bear up and steer right onward."

Patience is the capacity for being still when all around is tempest-tossed. Patience is the flower of fidelity. If fidelity is the activity of faith, patience is the condition of character resulting therefrom. It is that peace of heart under pressure of life which is so fair and fragrant a thing to us, and ever seems to give the heart of the Lord satisfaction and joy.

And yet again. "I know . . . that thy last works are more than the first." There had been progress and development resulting from this intermediate group of facts, the outward and evident activity of the church had broadened and deepened. Such was the Master's commendation, and very beautiful it is. How tenderly the Lord recognizes all the best

The Thyatira Letter

facts in the life of the church. How excellent a thing it would be if when, for any reason, we are called upon to criticize some assembly of the saints, we might take our Lord's pattern, and utter first our commendation. This He always did unless there were no word of commendation that could be uttered. In His messages we ever discover His recognition of excellent things.

But now we pass to the solemn words of this most mysterious epistle, the words of complaint. "But I have against thee, that thou sufferest the woman Jezebel." That is all. Nothing more. There is no other complaint against this church. The whole paragraph which follows from the middle of the twentieth verse to the end of the twenty-third contains simply the statement of the facts of the case, which demonstrate our Lord's right to complain against the church for suffering the woman. It cannot be over-emphasized that the sin of this church consisted in the fact that she raised no protest against the woman Jezebel, that she allowed an outsider to promulgate under her shelter the most terrible doctrine, with the most disastrous results. Jezebel did not belong to the church, She may have been a member of the congregation, even perhaps enrolled on the earthly list of the fellowship, but she had no living relation with the church because she did not belong to Christ. The church incurred a terrible responsibility by suffering her. Not the teaching, nor the result of the teaching did the Lord charge against the church, save as she becomes responsible for what she suffers. The wrong of this false toleration may be gathered from an examination of the woman, her work, and her judgment.

In attempting to consider the woman Jezebel, we are at once found in the presence of all kinds of questionings and doubts and interpretations. Is the whole language figurative? Does Jezebel stand for an idea, or was she actually a woman, exerting evil influences through pernicious teaching in Thyatira? These things perhaps cannot be finally or satisfactorily answered. The greatest probability is that there was an actual woman. The marginal rendering of the message to the angel is, "Thou sufferest thy wife Jezebel," and there are those who believe that this woman was indeed the wife of the angel of the church. Whether this be so or not, there can be little doubt of the existence of an actual woman. Whether her real name was Jezebel may be

The Thyatira Letter

doubtful. It is probable that when the Master named the woman, He borrowed a name from the Old Testament in order to light up the fact of her character, and the influence she was exerting.

Turn from these things that are doubtful, and let us examine the actual words of Christ. "Thou sufferest the woman Jezebel, which calleth herself a prophetess." What is a prophetess, and why is the statement made in this form, "she calleth herself a prophetess?" There can be very little doubt that the woman claimed to be an inspired woman, who had received some new revelation. Some vision or enlightenment had been granted to her, denied to the apostles, and she was promulgating this new teaching.

The result is carefully stated by the Lord in the words "she teacheth and seduceth." The result of the teaching was the seduction of the servants of God, and the teaching was made forceful because the woman claimed that she was an inspired messenger. The name that the Master uses in referring to her, suggests an analogy with her Old Testament prototype. Let us think for a moment of the Jezebel of old.

She was a daughter of the king of Tyre

and Sidon, avowedly a teacher and worshipper of Baal. This worship of Baal was Nature worship, and as is the case with all Nature worship, it had become utterly degraded. Coming into relationship with the king of Israel by marriage, we learn from the ancient history of God's people that she was not only his consort, but that she was associated with him in the government, with the result that she said in effect, 'Let us also set up the worship of Baal. I do not ask that the worship of Jehovah should be set aside, but by the side of it let us have opportunities for Nature worship.' Her method was that of uniting the two worships. The purpose in her heart was that of the setting aside of the worship of Jehovah for the worship of Baal. Of all the women seen in Old Testament history, none was more brilliant, more daring, more unscrupulous than Jezebel.

The name of this woman in the church at Thyatira drives us back to this woman of the old economy, and of her the Lord declares that she "teacheth and seduceth My servants to commit fornication, and to eat things sacrificed to idols." What was it that she was teaching? Nothing at the moment seems to be said on

The Thyatira Letter

the point, but presently when the Master is pronouncing His judgment, He gives us a clue to the character of the teaching. "But to you I say, to the rest that are in Thyatira, as many as have not this teaching, which know not the deep things of Satan, *as they say.*" What did the Lord mean by this "*as they say?*" He evidently refers to a claim set up within the teaching of Jezebel, that she had discovered some new deep hidden philosophy of life. Christ called it "the deep things of Satan." This new revelation by inspiration, the end of which was to show how in the heathen systems were deep philosophies, and the result of which was to seduce the servants of God into complicity with the outward corruptions of heathendom, Christ characterizes as the "deep things of Satan." It was evidently an attempt to graft on to Christianity as revealed in the Church, the mysteries of darkness by which Christianity was surrounded in that district. As there was the germ principle of Antinomianism dealt with in the church at Pergamum, so here there is the germ principle of the heresy of Gnosticism in the woman Jezebel. Here was an attempt made to fathom deep and underlying and unrevealed mysteries of life, and to make application of them under the name and sanction of the church, and the issue of the whole business was corruption.

Truly there is nothing new under the sun. The latest of all heresies which names itself by conjunction of words, Christian and Science, of all the facts concerning which it is profoundly ignorant, is but the galvanizing of a mummy, under the inspiration of yet another woman, calling herself a prophetess. This latter day manifestation, dealt with philosophically, might be treated as the amusement of a passing hour, but the terrible effect it is producing among the servants of God, should call the Church to new attention to our Lord's message to Thyatira, and the estimate it contains of His view of a church that suffers such awful teaching.

What then according to the Master's estimate was the result of this woman's teaching? It was a lowering of the standard of separation between the church and the world. One uses the very word with bated breath, for it is a terrible word. "She teacheth and seduceth My servants to commit fornication." In the prophecy of Hosea there is a startling revelation of the nature of spiritual fornication. It is God's estimate of the sin of those who

The Thyatira Letter

were betrothed to Him, when they return to the things from which they had turned to Him. People who should be satisfied with Christ, wholly possessed by Him, led by Him, taught by Him, are playing the harlot with the things that are against Him. The influence of the teaching of Jezebel was that the separated children of God, redeemed from the present evil world, called to separation from that world, were forming new alliances therewith, and the spirit of worldliness was spreading because of the toleration of the teaching of Jezebel. The members of the church at Thyatira were finding their way to the feasts in the heathen temple, eating the things sacrificed to idols, and descending even to the depth of the vices that ensued. The teaching which made this possible for them was not the teaching of Balaam, which said that the covenant was so sure and strong that sin could not break it. This denied the sinfulness of sin, affirming that within the things that seem to be evil are things of good. It was a practical denial of evil, in that it advocated union between the deep things, or mysteries of the outside world, and the mysteries which are the revelations of the Christian Church. And so the servants of God had become seduced by the teaching. First, the false teaching concerning the "deep things of Satan," and then the seduction following. His people went over to the forces which were against Him, and committed harlotry and fornication in the spiritual realm by using freedom, bestowed by Him, for the violation of His will. His charge against the church was that notwithstanding these terrible facts, she was silent and tolerant.

Then mark His words of judgment. These are introduced with a declaration of His patience, "And I gave her time that she should repent." Then follows a statement that reveals the Speaker, reveals Him as the Son of God, and reveals Him as the One Whose eyes are as a flame of fire. "She willeth not to repent of her fornication." No one else could have said that. He Who knows even these deep things of Satan, declares that the will is hardened and set against repentance, and then, and never until then does He pronounce judgment.

There is first a personal visitation. "Behold, I do cast her into a bed." The symbolism is graphic and forceful and terrible. It suggests that the woman, who has taught and seduced His servants, shall find her destruction in the midst of the very corruption which

The Thyatira Letter 125

she has created. More than that cannot be said.

Then follows the fact that others will share in the doom. "And them that commit adultery with her into great tribulation, except they repent of her works." The only way to escape the tribulation which He pronounces upon those who have been seduced, is that they shall repent of her works, and turn altogether from the things resulting from her teaching.

And then the last and final word in this connection "I will kill her children with death; and all the churches shall know that I am He which searcheth the reins and hearts."

This description of the woman, her sin, and her judgment lies in a paragraph in the midst of the epistle, recording our Master's reason for disapproval. The church's wrong was that this woman had been permitted. Some of the children of God had been seduced, and yet no protest had been raised. It was a false charity, permitting the teaching of the woman, somewhere and somehow under the patronage of the church itself. The whole church was not contaminated with the doctrine. Of it He said some of His sweetest and strongest things. But in a false charity the woman Jezebel had been suffered. The church had not with sufficient clearness announced the fact that she had no dealing with the heresy taught, that between the inspired truth of which the church was the pillar and the ground, and the hysterical teaching from the self-styled prophetess, there was no complicity, and could be no union.

Now let us turn to our Lord's words of counsel, full of encouragement and gracious promise. "But to you I say, to the rest that are in Thyatira." Thus to those who had not been influenced by the teaching, nor consented to its toleration, He said, "I cast upon you none other burden. Howbeit that which ye have, hold fast till I come." Did He mean that they were to hold fast the burden until He came? Assuredly He did. What then is the burden? The truth as once for all delivered to them; and by saying, "I cast upon you none other burden," He meant, Do not be led away by any new mysteries, or new perplexities, or new revelations. I have laid upon you the burden of truth sufficient for the moment. "I cast upon you none other burden." Any new revelation that men claim as from Me, receive it not. Any new philosophy of life that fails to harmonize with that declared, reject. "Howbeit that which ye have," the truth as revealed,

The Thyatira Letter 127

My law of life, that hold fast. Do not suffer anyone to teach something which I forgot to say! "I will cast upon you none other burden."

Carefully note this. There seems to be almost a play upon words in what Jesus said; there is certainly familiarity with their root meaning. He says, Those of you who have not this teaching, that "know not the deep things of Satan"—that word, "deep things" is the word βάθος, that is, the profundities of Satan. And He then says, "I cast upon you none other burden." That word "burden" is the word βάρος, which means an impression made. Both βάθος and βάρος spring from the original root βάσις. It is evident that He was speaking with an intimate knowledge of the history of the words, and indulging in a play upon them. It is as though He had said, These people are professing to discover some new *deep things,* which they will lay upon you. "I cast upon you none other *deep things.*" Herein is a great principle for the government of our intelligent life as Christian people. The thing claiming to be new, is therefore to be doubted. The message He has delivered is complete, the doctrine is enunciated, the mysteries are revealed, and whosoever, man or woman, would claim to reveal a new mystery, is the messenger of Satan.

And yet again " Hold fast till I come." How often this reference to His coming, and almost wherever found, it has some fresh light and meaning. It is as though He would say, Wait for the deeper things until I come. When I come I will unlock the mysteries, I will reveal the profundities. If I have not told you of them, it is because you cannot bear them yet. There are deep mysteries of life, and great and marvellous secrets, but you are not ready for their understanding. "I cast upon you none other burden." You have all you can bear. " Howbeit that which ye have, hold fast till I come." And then we shall know as we are known, and the mysteries, attempting to fathom which to-day we can find corruption only, will flame with light, and lead in the way of truth.

The closing promise and the crowning statement follow. "And he that overcometh, and he that keepeth My works unto the end, to him will I give authority over the nations: and he shall rule them with a rod of iron, as the vessels of the potter are broken to shivers; as I also have received of My Father." Notice the contrast. " Them that commit adultery with her into great tribulation, except they repent of *her* works." "He that overcometh, and he

The Thyatira Letter

that keepeth *My* works." This is the promise of a coming authority, an authority to be delivered to the saints, when they have held fast to the trust committed to them, until God's moment of consummation arrives.

"I will give him the morning star." We shall often walk in darkness. There will be many mysteries perplexing us. The burden we have is sufficient for the building of our character, for our growth in life, and ministry and works. The other things will wait. Presently He will give us the morning star. That expression only occurs three times in Scripture. In the book of Job, in the language of God, when He is causing His glory to pass before the astonished vision of His servant, He tells Job of the wonder-working age, when He laid the beams and wonders of Nature, and He says "When the morning stars sang together." This was the song of the principalities and powers in the heavenly places as they wrought in the spaces of new creation.

I go to the end of the Library, and I find that Jesus says, "I am the bright and the Morning Star." He is the Prince of creation, He is the First-born, and if we will but wait, and not follow the last false philosophy of impertinent attempt to discover hidden things, He will give us the morning star. We shall know the secrets of life, the deepest problems, and discover His Lordship in all.

How often has the Church of Christ imperilled her safety by giving undue heed to some new voice. I am growingly afraid of the men or the women who have seen a vision, and now feel called upon to declare it. Do not misunderstand me. I believe in visions. But let us before we speak of the vision be perfectly sure that it is not nightmare. The probability is that if you have a vision, you will not say much concerning it, but men will know that you have seen by the light that lingers on your face. Perfect light has shined upon man in Christ. With the shining of that light, all symbols and signs of the old covenant have passed, and the visions and the dreams have very largely ceased. The lower orders of material miracles have given place to the higher in the realms of spiritual triumph. Let us ever be careful how we give credence to a new voice. We must be loyal to Christ, and loyalty to Christ is loyalty to the inspired Word, and its mighty teachings. To deny Christ is to deny atonement, and to deny sin, and the only voice that denies these has learned its language and caught its tone in the deep things of Satan.

Is not the voice of Jezebel to be heard in our churches to-day in more ways than one? Is there not sounding all around us a cry as against separation? Is there not a terrible tendency in church life to deny that the Master calls us to places of peculiarity and loneliness in our loyalty to Him? We may still retain our church relationship, and our name Christian, and because of some new voice, eat of things sacrificed to idols, without defilement, and have easy absolution, not by blood, from the filth of fornication. Is it really popular to-day to call church members into the place of separation from worldliness? Is there not a greater eagerness than ever to find some doctrine by submission to which we can be rid of sin, while still keeping it?

Yet surely the New Testament is perfectly clear.
"Come ye out from among them, and
    be ye separate,
saith the Lord
    And touch no unclean thing;
    And I will receive you,
    And will be to you a Father,
    And ye shall be to Me sons and
        daughters,
saith the Lord Almighty.

"Who gave Himself for our sins, that He might deliver us out of this present evil world."

"If then ye were raised together with Christ, seek the things that are above, where Christ is, seated on the right hand of God."

"Who gave Himself for us, that He might redeem us from all iniquity, and purify unto Himself a people for His own possession."

"Be ye yourselves holy in all manner of living."

Through the whole New Testament the call is to separation, to peculiarity, to a clear line of demarcation between the Church and the world. I fear that the voice of Jezebel is yet tolerated, and that the children of God are being seduced. Things at which our fathers shuddered are to-day being introduced as necessary to the social and financial success of the Church. In the name of God and humanity, let us keep the line clear and sharp, and know on which side we stand. Any doctrine, any philosophy, that makes it easy to sin, whether by excusing it, minimizing its enormity, or denying its existence is of hell, and not merely are those held guilty who teach the doctrine and practise the sin, but that church also which is not clear and outspoken in its protests against sin. The church that suffers the woman is guilty.

THE SARDIS LETTER

"And to the angel of the church in Sardis write;
"These things saith He that hath the seven Spirits of God, and the seven stars: I know thy works, that thou hast a name that thou livest, and thou art dead. Be thou watchful, and stablish the things that remain, which were ready to die: for I have found no works of thine fulfilled before My God. Remember therefore how thou hast received and didst hear; and keep it, and repent. If therefore thou shalt not watch, I will come as a thief, and thou shalt not know what hour I will come upon thee. But thou hast a few names in Sardis which did not defile their garments: and they shall walk with Me in white; for they are worthy. He that overcometh shall thus be arrayed in white garments; and I will in no wise blot his name out of the book of life, and I will confess His name before My Father, and before His angels. He that hath an ear, let him hear what the Spirit saith to the churches." Rev. iii: 1-6.

VII

THE SARDIS LETTER

THERE is a marked change in our Lord's method of address to the church at Sardis. Hitherto He has commenced with words of commendation. Here He commenced with words of condemnation. In the other churches evil had not been the habit, but rather the exception, and therefore it was possible first to commend. Here the case is reversed, and no word of commendation is addressed to the church as a church.

The Lord addressed the church as "He that hath the seven Spirits of God, and the seven stars," and this commendation marks those aspects of His personality which characterize His dealing with a church in such condition. "He that hath the seven Spirits of God." This description indicates His fulness of power, and also His fulness of wisdom. The church for lack of life, is full of unfulfilled works, and the Lord approaches them in all the plenitude of His power and His wisdom. "He that hath . . . the seven stars." This symbol is suggestive at once of the perfection of ministry which He places at the disposal of the churches, and also therefore of His knowledge of all such ministry as the churches have received.

His complaint is startling and terrible. "I know thy works, that thou hast a name that thou livest, and thou art dead." With what changed emphasis we read the words "I know." The whole tone of it has been full of tenderness and comfort. Now it is a trumpet-blast of terror. "I know thy works." The church at Sardis is not devoid of works. Indeed it is so full of them as to give it a name of being alive. In all probability there was full and correct organization, the ordinances of the church were regularly observed. They gathered upon the first day of the week for worship. They contributed systematically to the necessities of the work. In brief, it is most likely that to all outward appearances they fulfilled the description of the early Church in the Acts of the Apostles, in that they "continued stedfastly in the apostles' doctrine, in the breaking of bread, and in fellowship, and in prayers." "Thou hast a name that thou livest." There can be but one signification in this statement of Christ. Nothing is lacking as to external manifestation, and

The Sardis Letter 137

yet Christ says "And thou art dead." He Who seeks first for the inward life, finds nothing to satisfy His heart in this church. Scaffolding is of no value to Him if the building be making no progress behind it. The whiteness of a sepulcher does not attract Him if within there be nothing but dead bones. He seeks always for the inward, and only for the outward as it continues to be the expression of the inward. The breaking of bread is nothing save as there is the spiritual feeding upon Himself. The meeting for worship is valueless save as through the externals, the soul passes into communion with Him. Gifts are not accepted when they are the mere observance of a duty, and not the expression of the heart's adoration. The life which expresses itself in love was absent, and so the church lacked what would be acceptable to Christ, and would satisfy for all the toil He had endured to win it for Himself. "Thou art dead." Flowers there may be, but of wax, poor imitations of the flowers of God which grow and bloom and shed their fragrance. The form of manhood may be there, and the garments in which the form is draped be gorgeous, and all the trappings speak of royalty, and yet the body be loathsome to Christ, for the eye lacks lustre, the arm is nerveless, the heart is still, death reigns and corruption is already holding high carnival.

"Thou hast a name that thou livest." That is to say, that there was everything in Sardis that would satisfy the outside observer. "And thou art dead." That is to say, there was nothing in Sardis that could satisfy the heart of Christ. This seems difficult to comprehend, but the explanation is to be found in the further words of Christ. "I have found no works of thine fulfilled. before My God." There was great promise, but no result, that is, nothing fulfilled before God. Was there no prayer? On earth there were prayers, but they did not reach the heavens. Were there no songs? In all likelihood, the music was correct and elaborate, but no harmony was heard in the heavenly temple. Were there no gifts? In all probability gifts were bestowed with unfailing regularity, but they were not registered in the treasury of the inner sanctuary. Everything stopped short of the inner temple. All kinds of Committee meetings attended, but nothing done, nothing finished, nothing fulfilled. Resolutions, and promises, and a great showing upon paper, but nothing reaching fruitage before God, nothing that satisfied the Divine heart, nothing that answered the Divine

The Sardis Letter

purpose. Outward forms, ceremonies, organization; but death reigned.

The essence of worship is that while it begins in the church, it takes hold upon heaven. If the hymn is simply a musical expression of pleasant feeling, there is no worship in it. But if upon the wings of sacred song our spirits find their way into the Holy of Holies, then that song is fulfilled before God. If the prayer we utter is a compilation of sentences, spoken for the fulfilment of duty, it is not prayer. But if the prayer, expressing a sense of need, finds its way above the mists and the mysteries of life, to the throne, it is fulfilled before God. If our gifts are bestowed that we may be kept square with duty, they are utterly refused in heaven. But if they express a sacrifice and a sympathy, though they be but small according to the arithmetic of men, they are counted of great worth in that temple where gifts are valued according to the givers.

In the church at Sardis there were plans, schemes, programmes, but nothing fulfilled before God, no growth into the likeness of Christ, no enlargement of the church through the propagation of the Christ-life, no compassion for souls, no fellowship with the sufferings of Christ. There were many things fulfilled before men; indeed, the church had come to the place where it lived before men rather than before God, more anxious in all probability about their reputation in Sardis than their reputation in heaven, more desirous for the good opinion of neighbouring churches, than for the commendation of the Head of the Church. "Thou hast a name," everything that will satisfy the craving for reputation, "and thou art dead," nothing that gladdens the heart of God.

Having thus in one swift sentence revealed the church's lack, He continues in words of gracious counsel. "Be thou watchful, and stablish the things that remain, which were ready to die: for I have found no works of thine fulfilled before My God. Remember therefore how thou hast received and didst hear; and keep it, and repent. If therefore thou shalt not watch, I will come as a thief, and thou shalt not know what hour I will come upon thee." And then omitting the next verse, "He that overcometh shall thus be arrayed in white garments; and I will in no wise blot his name out of the book of life, and I will confess his name before My Father, and before His angels." His words of counsel contain, first, advice to the church; secondly, an in-

The Sardis Letter

centive to obedience and a warning; and lastly, His promise to the overcomer.

"Stablish the things that remain." If the church was dead, what things remained? The unfulfilled things, the very forms and ceremonies which had given the church its name to live. Christ did not suggest that these people should put aside any of their externalities, but that they should fulfil them. They were not to cease assembling for worship, but they were to worship. They were still to send their help, and give their gifts, but these were to be the expressions of their devotion to their Lord, and not the price they paid for the good opinion of others. The forms were not wrong. They needed to be filled with power. The dry bones were necessary, but they needed to be clothed with flesh, and become instinct with life. The organization must not be neglected, but it should act in the power of vital force.

There can, I think, be no other understanding of this expression, "the things that remain." He cannot have reference to a faint life that needed revival, for He distinctly says "thou art dead." This part of the message is not for the few in Sardis, for to them He has a special word. No, it is rather that in tender grace, He recognizes the outward symbol, the unfulfilled things, the very forms and ceremonies that have been earth-bound, and He says, Strengthen them, stablish them, fill them to the full. Be no longer satisfied with externals.

That is ever Christ's message to the formalist. He does not ask that outward form should be given up, or helpful rite abandoned. He will not suggest the setting aside of any form or ceremony that in itself is helpful. He has no criticism for these things. He permits the music and the methods, always providing that they are expressive of the deeper fact of life. These things He hates when they become the grave-clothes wrapped about death. The true ideal of worship is that of man communing with God. Through what forms that worship expresses itself is of little moment. Christ does not call the church at Sardis to abandon these, but to stablish them by making them instinct with life.

Specially mark the significance of the words that follow, " which were ready to die." This is a solemn note of warning. It indicates the fact that even these outward forms will cease, unless there be behind them the throb of life. They are ready to die, as all that is merely outward perishes. The very things that remain, the outward forms and ceremonies, which give the church a name to live, are ready to perish if the heart and life have passed away. It is always but a step from formalism to rationalism, and if external things lack internal force, they themselves will crumble to decay, and presently there will remain in Sardis not even a church having a name to live.

No man can live long on ritual. How often has the Church had proof of this. Stretching over the hill-side yonder is a forest of mighty oaks, and among them I see one necessarily attracting attention by the magnificence of its form, and the splendour of its outward appearance. It is easily the king of the forest. But presently under stress of a sweeping storm that tree is bowed and broken. We approach, in wonder, to discover the reason, and find that through processes we did not observe, which were secret and silent in operation, an inward decay had long been at work. The life forces within had been weakened, and in the rush of the tempest the outward appearance was destroyed.

So also with the Church. When its inward life force has ebbed away into orthodox organizations, it is ready to die, to perish. In the sight of Christ it is dead already, though it has yet a name to live; and when dead in His sight it will surely soon be seen to be dead even by those among whom for the moment it has a name to live.

What is true of the Church is equally true of the individual. No man can become absorbed in the external to neglect of the inward and spiritual without being in danger of losing the external manifestation also. How often have we seen it! Men leave the plain and simpler forms of worship for outward magnificence of manifestation, hoping by these things to compensate for lack of spiritual power, and the next thing we hear of them is that they have abandoned their outward relation to the Church also. It is of little importance what the outward form may be, providing that the inner life is there, and that through the externalities it is finding full expression.

Works unfulfilled before God must sooner or later manifest their emptiness before men. Therefore let the things that remain, which were ready to die be stablished.

As an incentive to obedience, the Lord utters a solemn warning. "If therefore thou shalt not watch, I will come as a thief, and thou shalt not know what hour I will come upon thee." How differently the promise of

The Sardis Letter 145

His coming sounds under different circumstances of Church life and Church character. When sacred things lose power, precious things lose blessing. When faith is dead, hope becomes dread. In the early first love of Christian experience, the thought of the advent of Christ is a thought of hope. When that love is lost, and death reigns, that which is the brightest star in the firmament to the trusting heart becomes a dread of darkness. The promise which produces a thrill of joy, becomes a thought of terror to the men who have fallen out of harmony with the Lord and Master.

In Scripture the advent of Jesus is constantly described under two aspects. The last prophecy uttered before His first advent, has the same recognition of dual significance. "For, behold, the day cometh, it burneth as a furnace; and all the proud, and all that work wickedness, shall be stubble; and the day that cometh shall burn them up, saith the Lord of Hosts, that it shall leave them neither root nor branch." What a terrible announcement. But yet listen again, for the prophet proceeds without break, "But unto you that fear My name shall the sun of righteousness arise with healing in His wings; and ye shall go forth, and gambol as calves of the stall." What a contrast. On the one side a day of burning and destruction. On the other the sun rising with healing in its light. Are these two different advents? No, the difference is created by the condition of the people at the dawning of the day.

To those who work wickedness the day would be one of burning and destructive heat. To those who fear His name the day would be of healing, the dawning of the morning, the breaking of light. The sun has two effects. It will burn up the parched ground until it becomes like a cinder. A plant in such ground, devoid of water, will be killed by the heat; but if a tree be planted by the rivers of water, and its roots go down and take hold of the springs of life, the sun will be the messenger of health and growth and advancement.

So also with regard to the second advent. The church's attitude toward the doctrine is always a revelation of the church's spiritual condition; and the attitude of the individual soul toward the thought of the Lord's return is always a revelation of that soul's condition before God. If I have a name to live while I am dead, then His announcement "I will come!" is a thought of terror. But if I have

The Sardis Letter 147

life and love and loyalty, the promise of His coming is the promise of day break.

In referring to the second advent the apostle of love wrote, "And now, my little children, abide in Him: that, if He shall be manifested, we may have boldness, and not be ashamed before Him at His coming." Two attitudes towards His coming are here revealed, "boldness," "ashamed before Him." The difference is created by the condition of those who wait for Him. If abiding in Him, then at His coming we shall have boldness. If not abiding in Him, we shall be ashamed before Him.

This is a very searching test of our personal condition. If when we hear the coming of Jesus spoken of, it is as the voice of music in the soul, then are we fulfilling our works before God. If on the other hand, the mention of the possibility of His approach creates the desire to postpone that coming, it is because our relation to Him is formal rather than living. The soul that lives in Christ, and works with Him amid the defilement of a decadent age, never hears His message "Behold, I come quickly" without answering, "Even so come, Lord Jesus."

This announcement of His coming gives force to the word "Remember therefore how thou hast received and didst hear; and keep it and repent." If the church hear His warning, and repent, and watch, and stablish the things remaining, the promise of His coming will have in it no terror, but be a veritable gospel of hope. But if the church abide in the realm of formalism, having a name, but lacking life, then the declaration that He will come can produce nothing but fear.

To the overcomer the Master says " He that overcometh shall thus be arrayed in white garments; and I will in no wise blot his name out of the book of life, and I will confess his name before My Father, and before His angels." The man that overcomes is the one who remembers and repents. To such He promises the final robing, " He shall thus be arrayed in white garments," and a recognition in the final roll-call, " I will in no wise blot his name out of the book of life, and I will confess his name before My Father, and before His angels." The robing in white garments is symbolical not of the purity of Christ, but of the manifestation of the works of the saints, works purified by Christ, and revealed in the light of the Father's house; and the names of such, Christ will confess in the presence of His Father and of the holy angels.

The Sardis Letter

Then there is also that tender word of commendation almost a parenthesis, not spoken to the whole church as describing it, but of a remnant that have not passed under the condemnation. "But thou hast a few names in Sardis which did not defile their garments: and they shall walk with Me in white; for they are worthy." In the midst of the formalism of the many, there were a few who lived and fulfilled their works before God, who did not defile their garments, and to these the Master says, "They shall walk with Me in white for they are worthy." In Scripture the robing of the saint is ever an expression of the saint's own service and character. In the description of the white robed multitude in Revelation, it is said that their white robes are the righteousness of the saints, not the righteousness of God, but the righteousness of the saints. That is to say, that fidelity of character and of service shall presently have its outward manifestation.

Is not some very beautiful light thrown upon the thought by the fact of the transfiguration of Jesus? On the holy mount His raiment became white and glistening, and the glory which the wondering disciples beheld was that of the outshining of His own perfection which made even the homely garment that He wore, flash with the splendour of heaven's own whiteness. Those who on earth did not defile their garments, shall finally walk with Him in white. They shall come to the time when there shall be manifested in outward glory their inward loyalty to Christ.

The chief thought of the church in Sardis had been that of popularity, of having a name. A few had been supremely anxious to be approved of Him, and concerning them He says, one day they shall be manifested in the glory of their own fidelity. That which is visible now to the eye of Christ shall finally be seen to be beautiful by others.

There is an awful possibility threatening the life of all our churches, and the church at Sardis is an example of warning concerning it. It is a possibility, so subtle and insidious, that almost before knowing, the church may have drifted into the peril. It is that of a dead orthodoxy, a dead correctness. There may be flourishing finances, large numbers attending the services, varied and ever increasing organizations, correct expositions of truth, and yet the church may be dead. It may have a name to live. It may be such as will always be spoken of as a living church. Surrounding

The Sardis Letter 151

churches may flatter it, and it may even be deceived itself, and yet Christ may find in it no element of value. Such a statement as that, such a solemn and awful statement should lead us to ask in all seriousness, What are the true signs of life in the churches of Jesus Christ? If the presence of life may not be judged by these things, how may we know whether the church is living or dead?

The evidences of life are at least fourfold. In a living church there will be growth, compassion, union, and emotion.

There will be growth. The principle of life makes stagnation impossible. Growth in the individual character of the members, and growth in the membership of the church, not merely by accretion from without, but by expansion from within. That church is in a sorrowful condition that has added nothing to its membership through the propagative life forces of its own communion. The membership that only grows by the accident of removals and letters of introduction is in a terrible condition. If none are born again directly through the working of the church, we may almost certainly say that the church is dead. I say that in all seriousness, and without apology. I would be afraid to remain as pastor or member of a church if for any length of time there were none added to its fellowship upon confession of faith. In this matter the minister cannot be held wholly responsible. He may travail in birth for souls, but unless the church is in co-operative and living sympathy with him, there will be no result. But where the whole communion is serving in the power of a great life, then through the Sabbath School, through the varied agencies, through the living influence of individual members, the life will be propagated, and men and women will be gathered into the fellowship upon confession of faith. Whatever else may be true concerning the church, if there be no additions by new birth, the church is dead, though it have a name to live. Life is always propagative, and that is nowhere so actually and forcefully true as in the realm of Christianity.

Another sign of life is that of compassion. The true consciousness of the Church is the consciousness of the Christ, and the consciousness of the Christ is that of love. That church which has no heart of compassion for the lost, is dead. The suburban church that attempts to buy off its own personal responsibility by making donations to send men down to work in slums which it does not care itself to touch, is dead. Such responsibility can never be delegated. A church into which only one class or caste of persons gathers for purely selfish preservation, is a libel upon the very name of Christ. Every church should be an asylum for the lost, a refuge for the broken-hearted, a home of welcome for the harlot and the publican. In God's name let us take down the signs that label us churches of Christ if we have no compassion for such, and we have no compassion if it be not strong enough to overcome sentimental prejudices, which result from the mere accident of birth. A girl of good family and excellent opportunities, of much culture and refinement once said to me, when I asked her to visit in a neighbourhood characterized by suffering and sin, "I really could not do it. I am so sensitive. It makes me ill." God have mercy on such idle pretence. Can any be more sensitive than Jesus the Saviour? Can any refinement be superior to that of the perfect One of Nazareth? I blush with shame at a sensitiveness which proves an absence of compassion. It is only as we find our pride and prejudices whelmed in the strong sweep of His great love that we shall ever be prepared to touch the depraved.

154   A First Century Message

We are dead indeed if we lack compassion. If the love of Christ is shed abroad in the heart, and the church is swept by that love, there is utter forgetfulness of all the things that are objectionable. Refinement that refuses to relieve is nothing more than cultured paganism.

If there be love, there will also be union. Disintegration is a sign of death. If the church be filled with sections, and parties, and there be strifes and schism it is because of the lack of the life element. The prevalence of caste, and the existence of division within the borders of the church is a sure proof of its lack of life. In the full tide of Divine life, there is a constant consciousness of the unity of the Spirit.

And yet again. Where there is life there is emotion. Sometimes it seems as though the day has come when the highest type of life is supposed to be that which is most free from the possibility of emotion, and yet how false is the idea. I am alive, and because I am alive, I weep, I sing, I laugh, I mourn. It is the dead that have no tears, no laughter, no music, no mourning. I have no patience with the man who boasts that his religion lacks emotion. The church without tears and laughter, Christ has little use for. I put these things

The Sardis Letter

together for they are together. You cannot have tears without laughter. You never found a man capable of humour that was not also capable of sorrow. And no church that lacks joy has compassion. The church that lives, thrills with emotion, is full of laughter, and full of tears, perpetually breaks into song, and is silent again in the silence of pain. The experience of the individual members is realized within the great union.

If these things be lacking in the church, it is dead indeed. The signs of life are growth, compassion, union, and emotion. These being absent, there may be very many other things that give the church a name to live among men. But Christ, walking amid the lampstands, counts as nothing worth the externalities, and hungers for the growth, the compassion, the union, and the emotion that prove the life.

THE PHILADELPHIA LETTER

"And to the angel of the church in Philadelphia write;

"These things saith He that is holy, He that is true, He that hath the key of David, He that openeth, and none shall shut, and that shutteth, and none openeth: I know thy works (behold, I have set before thee a door opened, which none can shut), and thou hast a little power, and didst keep My word, and didst not deny My name. Behold, I give of the synagogue of Satan, of them which say they are Jews, and they are not, but do lie; behold, I will make them to come and worship before thy feet, and to know that I have loved thee. Because thou didst keep the word of My patience, I also will keep thee from the hour of trial, that hour which is to come upon the whole world, to try them that dwell upon the earth. I come quickly: hold fast that which thou hast, that no one take thy crown. He that overcometh, I will make him a pillar in the temple of My God, and he shall go out thence no more: and I will write upon him the name of My God, and the name of the city of My God, the new Jerusalem, which cometh down out of heaven from My God, and Mine own new name. He that hath an ear, let him hear what the Spirit saith to the churches." Rev. iii. 7-13.

VIII

THE PHILADELPHIA LETTER.

THIS is the second epistle which contains no word of complaint. To the church at Smyrna, suffering amid persecution and tribulation, His message was wholly of His own love and strength. Again to the church at Philadelphia, He has nothing save commendation, and the announcement of preservation from the period of calamity and trial which is coming to the whole earth.

The church being in true relationship to its Lord, He approaches it in His rightful character of the Supreme One Who directs the church's activity. "These things saith He that is holy, He that is true, He that hath the key of David, He that openeth, and none shall shut, and that shutteth and none openeth." Thus He announces three facts concerning Himself. Concerning His character; "He that is holy, He that is true:" concerning His official position; "He that hath the key of David:" concerning His administration; "He that openeth, and none shall shut, and that shutteth and none openeth." Between these things there is a close connection. His character of holiness and truth is His right to Kingship. He is, moreover, King by the official act of God as witness His holding of the key of David. And because He is King in character, and by appointment, He exercises His Kingly office, and administers the affairs of His Kingdom. The relation between these facts must be remembered.

First let us consider the Kingly character. "He that is holy, He that is true." The first marks the essential fact, and the second the relative; holy in character, true in action; holy in Himself, true in His government. The two statements give us two sides of the one essential fact. These two statements constitute the complete whole which creates the true Kingliness of Christ, and gives Him what all other kings have lacked, the Divine right of Kingship.

These two facets of the one fact are constantly revealed in New Testament thought. In the prophecy of Zacharias chronicled in Luke, in referring to the result of the coming of Christ it is said, that He should establish the people in "holiness and righteousness," holiness the hidden fact, righteousness its out-

The Philadelphia Letter

ward manifestation; the rightness of character and conduct. "He that is holy," that is, right in character. "He that is true," that is, right in conduct. Holy, and therefore in Himself royal; true, and therefore making others loyal. By His holiness of character and truth of conduct He creates a consciousness which demands the loyalty of those who find Him as their King. It is always impossible to be loyal in all the broadest sense of the great word to that which is other than royal, also in the broadest sense of the word. No man who loves purity can be loyal to impurity. No man that has his heart set upon holy things can be loyal to that which is unholy. Loyalty must be the outcome of royalty. The royalty of earth is created by the accident of birth, or by the questionable right of conquest, and expresses itself in trappings and dwellings. Christ's right to Kingship rests upon the bedrock of character. He and He alone is King by Divine right, because He is holy, He is true.

The second Psalm announces the fact of God's appointment of a King.

"Yet have I set my King
Upon My holy hill of Zion.
I will tell of the decree:

The Lord said unto Me, Thou art My Son;
This day have I begotten Thee.
Ask of Me, and I will give Thee the nations for Thine inheritance,
And the uttermost parts of the earth for Thy possession."

The twenty-fourth Psalm reveals the character of that King.

"Who shall ascend into the hill of the Lord?
And who shall stand in His holy place?
He that hath clean hands, and a pure heart;
Who hath not lifted up his soul unto vanity,
And hath not sworn deceitfully.
He shall receive a blessing from the Lord,
And righteousness from the God of His salvation."

"I have set My King upon My holy hill of Zion." "Who shall ascend into the hill of the Lord? He that hath clean hands and a pure heart." This God-appointed King comes to the church at Philadelphia, and speaks of the deepest fact which constitutes His right to Kingship, "I am He that is holy."

And then He declares the necessary sequence, "He that is true."

He then proceeds to announce that His position is official. "He that hath the key of David." In Isaiah's description of Eliakim

The Philadelphia Letter 163

the son of Hilkiah, already referred to in another connection, it is written, " I will clothe him with Thy robe, and strengthen him with Thy girdle, and I will commit Thy government into his hand: and he shall be a father to the inhabitants of Jerusalem, and to the house of Judah." That is, government based upon life and upon resource. It is then added " And the key of the house of David will I lay upon his shoulder; and he shall open, and none shall shut; and he shall shut, and none shall open." From that prophecy the Lord quotes the words " He that hath the key of David," and thus claims its fulfilment in His own Person. He it is, to Whom God has committed His government, of which fact the key is the symbol and the sign.

And then in the last place He declares the fact of His administration. " He that openeth, and none shall shut, and that shutteth and none openeth." Let it be most particularly noted that Jesus did not say " He that can open and none can shut, and that can shut, and none openeth." That is obviously true, but He said something far stronger. He did not make a declaration of ability, but of activity. Not merely that He held an executive position, but that He was executing the work. "He that openeth, and none shall shut, and that shutteth and none openeth." This is not a distinction without a difference, but a difference with a distinction. Philadelphia was a church like the other churches of the time, existing in the midst of the corruption of paganism, and surrounded by forces which perpetually threatened to overwhelm these assemblies gathered around the risen One. To it however the Lord comes, announcing Himself in all the Kingly majesty of actual administration, "He that openeth, and none shall shut, and that shutteth and none openeth."

These words should bring to us a great sense of confidence and safety, notwithstanding all the appearances which appal us. He is God's King to-day, and though for a while man rejects Him, He nevertheless holds the reins of government, sitting upon the holy hill of Zion, King by right of character, King, as witness the key of office which He holds, He moreover acts in perpetual administration. He opens to-day, and He shuts to-day. Amid all the fret and restlessness of the age He is moving toward the final order, and that through the mysteries that enwrap us. Presently the crisis will arrive, and then the process will be vindicated. Let us ever comfort our hearts also with the threefold truth, of His character, "He that is holy, He that is true;" of His official position, "He that hath the key of David;" and of His actual administration, "He that openeth, and none shall shut, and that shutteth and none openeth."

In examining the commendation, a little care must be taken to notice the structure. "I know thy works (behold, I have set before thee a door opened, which none can shut), and thou hast a little power, and didst keep My word, and didst not deny My name." The words "Behold, I have set before thee a door opened, which none can shut," being in parenthesis, must be omitted from the commendation. Of course these words cannot be altogether omitted, neither would it be wise to place them anywhere but where the Lord has placed them. The commendation then consists in this statement, "I know thy works . . . that thou hast a little power, and didst keep My word, and didst not deny My name." Now in the parenthesis in the middle of that commendation comes the declaration concerning the opened door. The question arising is as to whether the Lord meant to say, that because they had kept His word, and not denied

His name, He had opened a door; or that, having opened the door, they had kept His word and had not denied His name. Without desiring to dogmatize upon what must be a somewhat difficult matter, let me say that I hold the latter view, that the open door is not a reward for fidelity, but the opportunity in which this church has proved its faithfulness. The statement of reward comes further on in the epistle. It is as though the Lord had said, I set before you a door opened, which none could shut, and I know your works, you had a little power, and didst keep My word, and didst not deny My name. He opened the door in front of them, and they passed through it and filled the opportunity. He opened the door, and they, though having but little power, were yet true to His word, and loyal to His name. It is evident then that the commendation must be considered wholly in the light of the statement concerning the open door.

What this open door was locally, it is impossible to state. We cannot go back and examine in detail the opportunity which the Lord gave the church. In all probability however it was some special opening for missionary enterprise. There is almost certainly a connection between the announcement of the Kingly char-

The Philadelphia Letter 167

acter of Christ and His opening of the door. It is "He that holdeth the key of David," which is the insignia of Kingship, Who has opened the door, and the suggestion is that of a passport given to His dominions for the transaction of His business. In the second Psalm already quoted of the announcement of the appointment of the King, the Divine promise concerning the King is made,

"Ask of Me, and I will give Thee the nations for Thine inheritance,

"And the uttermost parts of the earth for Thy possession."

The key opens the territory of the King. He Who held the key had set before the church a door opened. He had given them entrance to some other of His dominions for the transaction of His business. The opening of the door is the King's governmental preparation of the pathway, along which His messengers are to run to do His biddings, to herald His Gospel, to win His dominion for Himself. The opening of the door is the exercise of His executive right.

Turn for a moment from the immediate and local application of these words. Let us think of them as the statement of a great principle. How wondrously in every successive century

168 A First Century Message

has the King opened the doors before His Church. In spite of human opposition, and human hatred, He has unlocked and flung wide open the doors of opportunity before His faithful people. Never has this been more conspicuous than in the past century. It is not for us here to stay to illustrate the truth. Those who would follow the thought should obtain Dr. Arthur T. Pierson's book, "The Modern Mission Century," one of the most thrilling romances ever written since the first chapter in the history of the open doors, called the Acts of the Apostles. The message of the book will cheer the heart, and nerve the arm.

What the particular opening for the church at Philadelphia was, we have no means of knowing. The fact of value revealed is that there came to a church which was neither great nor strong, an opportunity which the church recognized and filled.

But who are these that enter through the open door? Mark well His description. Jesus did not say to this church at Philadelphia, Thou art strong, but "Thou hast a little power." But they were faithful to the opportunity in that they kept His word and did not deny His name. That is the true principle of success in Christian service. The greatest rewards that will ever come to churches or to men will be bestowed, not according to the greatness of the strength they had, or the greatness of the opportunity as it appeared to men, but according to fidelity to opportunity, and full use of the measure of strength possessed. The measure of strength was small, but entering the open door the church made use of all in loyalty to His word, and in maintaining the honour of His name. In this twofold statement there is a revelation of the secret of success in all service, the keeping of the word, and loyalty to the name. Of the first of these there is a double explanation.

The word of Christ is not kept merely by defending its letter but by realizing its spirit in obedience to its teaching. No man keeps the word of Christ in duty unless he keeps it as doctrine; and yet no man keeps the word of Christ as doctrine unless he possess it in all the details of duty. If life is to be according to the will of the King, there must be knowledge of His teaching. Knowledge of the teaching is only evident as life harmonizes therewith. There is great force in the word "keep."

The other phrase marks the fact which is correlative, "Thou didst not deny My name."

Holding the word of Christ must issue in unswerving loyalty to His name. Wherever there has been a tendency to undervalue the word, there has resulted the peril of insulting the name by degrading the personality. During recent years there has gone forward within the Church a certain kind of criticism of the words of Christ until we are not surprised, while strangely startled, that to-day the name of Jesus is being assailed by those who are questioning the essential facts concerning His Person and His nature. One hears of those who suggest that perhaps after all the story of miraculous conception is mythic. This is the necessary corollary of speaking of His words as partaking of the ignorance of His age. And such failure to keep the word and maintain the name inevitably reacts upon the Church in her fitness for service. His claim of Kingship is inseparably bound up with the miracles of His nature, and the authority of His speech. To deny these is to neglect the open doors. Infinitely better to have a little power, and use it within the doors He opens in loyalty to His teaching and Himself, than to have much power and use it as abetting the work of those who, robbing Him of His dignity, hinder His coming into His Kingdom,

The Philadelphia Letter 171

In passing to the Lord's counsel to this church, we notice that He emphasizes His administration. " Behold, I give of the synagogue of Satan, of them which say they are Jews, and they are not, but do lie; behold, I will make them to come and worship before thy feet, and to know that I have loved thee." Recognizing the difficult conditions under which this church has borne its witness, He declares His administrative activity, first with regard to the synagogue of Satan. This reference is of interest in as much as it closely resembles the Lord's reference in His other epistle without complaint, that to the church at Smyrna. He then said " I know thy tribulation, and thy poverty, and the blasphemy of them which say they are Jews, and they are not, but are a synagogue of Satan." In writing to Philadelphia, there is no such detailed declaration, but the passing reference creates the idea that there were conditions, calculated to hinder the church at Philadelphia, similar to those which hindered and brought tribulation to the church at Smyrna. There the Jewish synagogue had stirred up a pagan population to oppose the work of the church. It is likely that something of the kind had also happened in Philadelphia. Concerning such

He announces that the synagogue of Satan is yet to be compelled to recognize the church, " I will make them to come and worship before thy feet, and to know that I have loved thee." This is not the language of a great anger, nor that of vindictive administration. His ancient people who are hindering the work, are yet to be brought to the feet of the church, to learn how He has loved her. These administrative facts all lie in the realm of that great crisis, His second advent. To the church He says " Because thou didst keep the word of My patience, I also will keep thee from the hour of trial, that hour which is to come upon the whole world, to try them that dwell upon the earth." Recognizing the faithfulness of His people, He promises them exemption from the tribulation which is to come. While that promise may have had its partial fulfilment in the escape of the church at Philadelphia from some wave of persecution that swept over the district, its final fulfilment will undoubtedly be realized by those who, loyal to His word, and not denying His name, shall be gathered out of the world at His second coming before the judgment that must usher in the setting up of His Kingdom on the earth.

" I come quickly " is the great announce-

The Philadelphia Letter 173

ment which unlocks the meaning of this promise of exemption from coming tribulation. There can be no interpretation of the administration by which He shall bring the synagogue of Satan to the feet of the church, or of the church's being saved from tribulation save the thought contained in the announcement, " I come quickly."

In these words the Lord does for the church at Philadelphia what He has done for the Church again and again. He directs their attention to His second advent as the goal and crisis of victory. Through all the years of service the Church should ever wait for Him, hearing constantly the sound of His voice " I come quickly."

In view of that promise, consider the Master's declaration of the present responsibility of the church. "Hold fast that which thou hast, that no one take thy crown." To the church at Sardis He said the same thing, and yet how different the value and application of the announcement. To them it was a warning. To these it is a promise. To the church that was dead, it was a proclamation, calculated to startle them into obedience. To the church exercising its little strength in fulfilment of His gracious will, it was a declaration calculated to comfort them in obedience. Thus again it is evident that the doctrine of the advent of Jesus affects persons according to the condition of their life. One church is threatened, another is comforted by the announcement of His coming.

In the little while that lies between the present moment and His advent, He marks their responsibility in the words "Hold fast that which thou hast." What had they? A little power, His word, His name, His promise of return. These they were to hold fast, and the reason, "that no one take thy crown." The crown referred to was that of reward for service. He had opened the door. They in little power had entered in and had fulfilled His will. He knew their works, that they had kept His word and did not deny His name. He had no complaint to make of them. He Himself was coming, and at His coming they would have their crowning. Not the crowning but the conflict is for to-day, but so surely as the conflict is maintained, and the things now possessed held fast, the crowning must come.

Then lastly notice His promise to the overcomer. "He that overcometh, I will make him a pillar in the temple of My God, and he shall go out thence no more: and I will write upon him the name of My God, and the name of the city of My God, the new Jerusalem, which cometh down out of heaven from My God, and Mine own new name." The overcoming referred to in this case is not that of some evil in the church, but of the forces which are outside, and these will be finally overcome at His advent. As He has been speaking of that advent as the crisis at which all the rewards He promises will be bestowed upon the church, His promise to the overcomer is here that of those conditions of life to which they shall pass beyond that advent.

First He promises them position, "I will make him a pillar in the temple of My God." That is finality. The Bible does not speak of men as being pillars in His temple while on earth. Sometimes we have prayed for our children that they may become pillars in the house of God, and that will be, by and by, always providing that here they are trees of the Lord's planting by the rivers of water. Then yonder they will have a position conspicuous and abiding, based upon the fact of their approximation to the character of God.

Then secondly, "I will write upon him the name of My God," this indicating the fact of likeness, and the reason of the position of prominence.

And yet again, a definite and specific reward. "I will write upon him . . . the name of the city of My God, the new Jerusalem, which cometh down out of heaven from My God." Those who have the right within that city, of permanent dwelling upon the basis of character, are not to be there as foreigners or aliens, but as those who have the city's freedom, that freedom being the recognition of their overcoming.

And yet once more, "I will write upon him . . . Mine own new name." What strange and mystical statement is this? In the nineteenth chapter of this book of Revelation there is another reference to it. "He hath a name written, which no one knoweth but He Himself." There are yet honours for Jesus unrevealed, and these are signified in that new name. This then is the name that He will write upon the overcomer. He will share with him all His honours and rewards. There is to be the most perfect oneness between the overcomer and the King. To suffer with Him will be to reign with Him o'er all the territory. To enter the door He opens to-day is to walk with

The Philadelphia Letter 177

Him in all the spacious realms o'er which He yet must reign.

In this great and gracious promise to the overcomer, mark the reiteration of Christ's personal pronoun. "I will write upon Him the name of *My* God, and the name of the city of *My* God, the new Jerusalem, which cometh down out of heaven from *My* God." He came to do the will of His Father. He became the King upon the basis of the perfections of that will. And even in the unutterable anguish of the hour of His forsaking, there was still marked the relationship between Him personally and His Father, for even then He said "My God, My God, why hast Thou forsaken Me?" As He looks on to the ultimate triumph, all for Him lies within the fact of His relationship to God, and this is marked by that gracious word "My God."

To those who in little power, yet fulfil His purpose, He will give, as the reward of service, association with Himself in that union with His Father, which is the full glory and the final centre of perfect government.

From this study there are certain abiding lessons to be remembered. The first is a word of comfort, the word that reminds us of the present administration of Christ. Oh, that we may turn back to our work with the music of that thought ever sounding in our hearts. Our crowning may depend on our fidelity, but God's ultimate victory depends upon the King Whom He has set on His holy hill. Let there be no moment in which we imagine that He has either lost ground, or abandoned any part of the territory committed to Him. He cannot fail nor be discouraged till He have accomplished the uttermost purpose of His God, and though at times our eyes may fail to trace the method of His administration, let our hearts be ever comforted by remembering "He . . . openeth, and none shall shut, and He shutteth and none openeth." If we are not able to see how He opens or how He shuts, it matters little. The fact is full of infinite and inexpressible comfort. God's anointed King, though for a time hidden from the eyes of men, is carrying on His government. As of old, David the anointed king of Israel was for a time exiled from his kingdom, and took refuge in cave Adullam, so for to-day Christ is earth's rejected King, but He is still God's anointed King.

The story of Adullam is full of significance. David, refused by his people, went up to the fastness in the mountains, and there three classes of people gathered round him, men in debt, men in danger, and men that were discontented. Not of much count in the eyes of the nation. In all probability it was looked upon as a happy exodus when they left for the cave. And yet how wonderful the story of their relation to David, and its results. Contact with him turned them into mighty men. The story of David and his mighty men is indeed a romance. The raw material was surely as poor as ever gathered to a man, but than the finished product there has seldom been anything finer.

In process of time the glad day dawned when David left Adullam, and came to his crowning. Concerning that crowning a statement full of significance is made, " These all came to Hebron of one heart to make David king."

> "Our Lord is now rejected,
> And by the world disowned,
> By the many still neglected,
> And by the few enthroned."

But He is gathering to Himself a company of people in debt, in danger, and discontented, and those who have thus gathered to Him in the days of His rejection are by that contact and comradeship being transformed into His mighty men, and presently the morning will break when we shall gather with one heart to make Jesus King. Oh, take heart. Let there be fewer dirges sung in the sanctuary, and more pæans of praise. Let us have done with the lamentations of hope deferred, and putting on our garments of beauty, rise from the dust, and believe in our King. He at this moment holds the reins, and swaying the sceptre, administers the affairs of the Kingdom of God.

Such is the comfort to be gathered from this epistle. Then there follows a solemn word, marking our responsibility "Hold fast that which thou hast." Opposition is not over, Satan still has a synagogue. Open doors—and never had the Church such open doors as she has at this moment—open doors do not make strenuous fidelity unnecessary, but more than ever necessary. One of the most terrible facts of the present moment is that the Master is unlocking the doors all around, but the Church is not entering them as she should. Blindness to the fact is utterest folly. A great door and effectual is opened before the Church in India, that land of fascinating problems, and splendid opportunity. There we have undermined the false faiths by educational methods. At the present moment there are multitudes of men in that land, who have discovered the falsity of the faith of their fathers, and are now waiting for something else, and the Church is slow to bring to them the Evangel of the risen Christ. How terrible a thing it is to have taken away a faith, and yet not to be ready immediately to supply the lack. And India is but one instance. Surely never was it so true that the fields are white unto harvest but the labourers are few.

The Church should stand ready before every door, so that the moment it is open, she may occupy the territory for Christ. When will those who prosecute the commerce of heaven, manifest the same wisdom as that of the merchant princes of the earth? If the Church is thus to be ready and responsive to the call of the King she must hold fast His word, and not deny His name. Alas, that we have too often allowed things essential to be neglected, while we have been dealing with things of minor or of no importance. Back to the word, back to the name. Then will the Church be what God intends she should be, " fair as the moon, clear as the sun, terrible as an army with banners."

The final word of value from the study is that the test of the Church's loyalty to Christ is not the measure of her manifestation before men, but her fidelity to the opportunity her Lord creates. Infinitely better to have a little power only, all used for Christ, than much strength bestowed in other ways. If He have opened the door, then let us go through in all the strength we possess, remembering that our all, with the all of all the rest, shall make His all, that is, "the nations for His inheritance, and the uttermost parts of the earth for His possession."

THE LAODICEA LETTER

"And to the angel of the church in Laodicea write;

"These things saith the Amen, the faithful and true witness, the beginning of the creation of God, I know thy works, that thou art neither cold nor hot: I would thou wert cold or hot. So because thou art lukewarm, and neither hot nor cold, I will spew thee out of My mouth. Because thou sayest, I am rich, and have gotten riches, and have need of nothing; and knowest not that thou art the wretched one and miserable and poor and blind and naked: I counsel thee to buy of Me gold refined by fire, that thou mayest become rich; and white garments, that thou mayest clothe thyself, and that the shame of thy nakedness be not made manifest; and eye-salve to anoint thine eyes, that thou mayest see. As many as I love, I reprove and chasten: be zealous therefore, and repent. Behold, I stand at the door and knock: if any man hear My voice and open the door, I will come in to him, and will sup with him, and he with Me. He that overcometh, I will give to him to sit down with Me in My throne, as I also overcame, and sat down with My Father in His throne. He that hath an ear, let him hear what the Spirit saith to the churches."--Rev. iii: 14-22.

IX

THE LAODICEA LETTER

THIS last of the letters to the churches is in some sense saddest of them all, yet in other respects, it is most full of exquisite beauty. In every other epistle we find some word of commendation. Here there is absolutely none. This very fact seems to account for some of the tenderest and most wonderful words uttered by the Lord in the whole series. It is impossible to study this message without seeming to feel the heartbeat of the Son of God, and in none of the letters has there been more evident the yearning compassion of the Divine heart.

Very little is known of the church at Laodicea. We have no account of its planting, but there are certain references to it in the New Testament which may throw some light on its history. It is certain that the church was known to Paul, and it is most probable that he visited it. The latter position is of course open to question. Very much depends on the view taken concerning his imprisonment. If the confidence expressed in the letter to the Philippians was fulfilled that he would again visit his children, it is quite probable that among the rest, he would see Laodicea. The references he makes to the church are most interesting in the light of this message of Jesus.

In his letter to the church at Colosse there are no fewer than four references to the church at Laodicea. First in the second chapter, verses 1-3. "For I would have you know how greatly I strive for you, and for them at Laodicea, . . . that their hearts may be comforted, they being knit together in love, and unto all riches of the full assurance of understanding, that they may know the mystery of God, even Christ in Whom are all the treasures of wisdom and knowledge hidden." It is thus evident that while writing to the church at Colosse, he has in mind the church at Laodicea.

In the fourth chapter of the same epistle, in referring to Epaphras, the apostle says, "For I bear him witness, that he hath much labour for you, and for them in Laodicea." It is well to remember in passing that the labour of Epaphras was that of prayer. In the fifteenth verse of the same chapter he writes "Salute

The Laodicea Letter

the brethren that are in Laodicea," and yet again in the sixteenth verse, " And when this epistle hath been read among you, cause that it be read also in the church of the Laodiceans; and that ye also read the epistle from Laodicea."

Now these references show us very clearly one or two things. The apostle was acquainted with the church, and undoubtedly was interested in it. There was some kind of connection between it and the church at Colosse. In all probability they were geographically contiguous. It is quite conceivable that they were related to each other as mother and daughter, the church at Colosse founding the church at Laodicea, or being founded by it. It is moreover evident that there was interest and fellowship existing between them so that when Epaphras, a member of the church in Colosse laboured in prayer, that they of that fellowship might stand perfect and complete in all the will of God, he also included in his petitions the sister church at Laodicea.

Moreover it is probable that the apostle wrote to the church at Laodicea a special letter which has not been preserved, having most likely no perpetual value, for he distinctly charges the church at Colosse that the letter to the church at Laodicea is to be read to them also.

The apostle's interest in the church at Laodicea is marked in the first place by his prayer for them as for those at Colosse, that "their hearts may be comforted they being knit together in love, and unto all riches." The one great peril threatening the church at Laodicea was its wealth, and it may safely be inferred that the apostle saw the peril and prayed that "their hearts might be comforted, they being knit together in love, and unto all riches of the full assurance of understanding, that they may know the mystery of God even Christ," that is to say, he desired for them that they might have the true wealth, knowing as he probably did, that they were already possessed of much earthly wealth.

In the Authorized Version we have another reference to the church at Laodicea, which has been omitted from the Revised. It occurs at the close of the first letter to Timothy, and is of the nature of a note. "The first to Timothy was written from Laodicea which is the chiefest city of Phrygia, Pacatiana." That note of course presupposes that Paul was set free from the imprisonment during which he wrote, and that he visited this church, and

The Laodicea Letter

while among them wrote to Timothy who subsequently joined him, having been left in charge of the church at Ephesus. Our Revisers have omitted that statement, believing that there is no sufficient authority for it.

This much however, is certain that the church at Laodicea was known to the apostle, that he was deeply interested in it, and that it had some intimate fellowship with the church at Colosse.

In addressing Himself to this church, the Lord uses descriptive words, which at once arouse interest, and arrest attention. "These things saith the Amen, the faithful and true Witness, the Beginning of the creation of God." Here is nothing which symbolizes His manifested splendour. This is rather a declaration of His essential glory. The description creates a contrast. To abject failure He addresses Himself as the One incapable of failure. The statement is threefold; positive, relative, and declarative of authority. It is a profound proclamation of authority based upon the facts which are the cause and reason of all things.

First the positive statement, "These things saith the Amen." Secondly, the relative declaration, "the faithful and true witness."

Thirdly, the authoritative proclamation "the beginning of the creation of God."

He that is "the Amen." This word has come from the Hebrew without translation, and to understand its value, we must seek to know its original meaning in that language. The root meaning is that of nursing, or building up, and the derived meaning in perpetual use to-day is that of something stablished, built up sure, positive. The word therefore takes us back to God as the nursing Mother and expresses the truth of the absolute stability and the actual correctness of everything that God has thought, and spoken, and done. It is an essential word, "the Amen." All truth lies within its compass as to certainty. As a title of Christ it is equivalent in value to the statement which He made when he said " I am the truth." It must ever be remembered that He did not say " I teach the truth," nor, " I declare the truth," nor " I explain the truth," but " I am the truth." Here we have the same thought put in a form, almost more august and splendid. He that is "the Amen," the essential truth, truth expressed in a Person, truth from which there can be no appeal. The Amen is the conclusion, because it is the finality of nourishment, the perfection of edification, the

The Laodicea Letter

last word, the end, to which nothing can be added. So Christ approaching this church declares in the first phase of declaration that from Him there can be no appeal. He is the Certainty, the Finality, the Ratification, the ultimate Authority, the Amen.

Then follows the relative statement of the same great fact. "He is the faithful and true witness." He is that, because He is the Amen. He is that, because He is the truth. He is the Amen, even though He never speak. He is the Truth, if He utter no word. But now that the truth has been spoken by Him it is a faithful and true witness that He has borne. He is the faithful and true Witness of God and of the Church. When He speaks there is no exaggeration, and no minimizing. What he says is faithful and true because He is faithfulness and truth. What He says will be exactly true, because He is in Himself absolute truth, and there is nothing beyond Him in all the realm of truth.

The witness concerning all things in Him will be faithfulness and truth. He is the only One through Whom this perfect witness can be spoken. The church at Laodicea had failed in witness. Its condition had eclipsed the essential light that should have been shining in the darkness around, and the Master comes to it and addresses it as the faithful and true Witness. He is about to strip it of all the false appearance which deceives the eyes of many, but which cannot deceive Him. As in the old economy, by its last messenger, Jehovah said He would be a swift Witness against the sorcerers and evil doers, the witness of truth against evil, the One Who would drag the evil into the light of truth, so here as He comes to unmask the failure of the Laodicean people, He announces Himself as the One Who will neither exaggerate the condition, nor permit anything of it to remain hidden.

Then the last phrase brings us back into the sublimity of majesty. As we read it, we are impelled to worship. " The beginning of the creation of God." Having noticed the reference to Laodicea in Colossians, it becomes interesting to read Colossians in the light of Laodicea, and to notice how this very expression, " the beginning of the creation of God " is one of the pillars upon which the truth of the Colossian epistle rests. In that sublime and matchless statement concerning the glories of Christ, occurring in the first chapter of Colossians, verses fifteen to eighteen, these words occur, " Who is the image of the invisible God,

The Laodicea Letter 193

the Firstborn of all creation, for in Him were all things created, in the heavens, and upon the earth, things visible and things invisible, whether thrones or dominions or principalities or powers; all things have been created through Him, and unto Him; and He is before all things, and in Him all things hold together, consist." This betokens rank and right lying behind all other. If the heart ever questions the Deity of Christ it is well to go back and ponder this great statement. It is impossible to retain this in the Bible if Christ be anything less than God, and all the sublimity of these declarations lies in the suggestion within this title.

Approaching the church at Laodicea He comes as the One Whose rank is infinitely beyond that of priest, prophet, or king. He speaks with the authority of cause and creation. Wherever the eye rests, whatever the mind is conscious of, is as to first cause the work of Christ. His footprints may be tracked through all creation, and every blush of beauty reveals the touch of His finger. There are no flowers but have in them witness to Him, no marvellous and majestic landscape entrancing the vision of men but that sings the solemn anthem of His power and His beauty. In all the precision of created things, the rolling seasons, the dawn of day, and the westering of the sun, in the emergence of Spring, from its garment of Winter, its procedure into the splendour of Summer, and its gorgeous robing in Autumnal glory is to be discovered the power of the Christ.

Thus coming to a church conceited because of its wealth and independence. He sublimely announces His wealth and independence. If this church had but ears to hear, how it must have blushed with shame as the tawdriness of its wealth became apparent in the blinding splendour of His, and as the blasphemy of its independence was manifest, as the only One of independence declared Himself as the origin of all things. He speaks to them not as the King of a section, not as the One Who enunciates laws for one realm of the universe, but as the beginning of creation, the Cause and the Creator, Who is King of all creation, and enunciates for all the laws which condition life.

To the church at Laodicea, lifeless, indifferent, cool, He speaks as the One Who is the Source of all life, the infinite Energy, the beginning of the creation of God.

In this capacity of infinite majesty He

The Laodicea Letter

speaks no single word of commendation. Many are the words of hope He utters. He has not lost all hope even for this fearful failure at Laodicea. But there is no commendation. His counsel and complaint run close together, alternating through all the message. Let us select the complaint, considering it first, and then passing to attention to His counsel.

Three brief statements indicate the Lord's complaint. First " Thou art," and then " Thou sayest," and yet again, " Thou art." In the first He describes the general condition of the church. In the second He describes the church as the church thinks it is. In the third He reveals in minute and detailed truth the actualities.

First His vision of the church as to its spirit, and not as to its externalities, then a revelation of the church's belief concerning itself, and then the contrast, terrible and startling of His view of the church, even as to details.

" I know thy works, that thou art neither cold nor hot." Such is the spiritual condition as He declares it. " Thou sayest, I am rich, and have gotten riches, and have need of nothing." That was their consciousness. " Thou art the wretched one and miserable and poor and blind and naked, and thou knowest it not." That is their detailed condition in contrast with their supposed condition. These descriptions form our Lord's complaint.

"Thou art neither cold nor hot . . . thou art lukewarm." Let us take these words and attempt to see what they really indicate. "Cold," frozen, the thought of temperature lowered by evaporation lies within the word. "Thou art not frozen." The church was not characterized by utter indifference. "Hot," boiling. "Thou art not boiling." The church was not characterized by fervent heat. It was not utterly indifferent. It had no fervent zeal. What then is the condition? Lukewarm, and we may with perfect accuracy render the word tepid. Thou art not frozen, thou art not boiling, thou art tepid. If there is anything abhorrent to the heart of Christ it is a tepid church. He would rather have the church frozen. I did not say that. He did. "I would thou wert cold." He would rather have the church boiling. "I would thou wert . . . hot." But this condition of being tepid is utterly repugnant to Him. No emotion, no enthusiasm, no urgency, no passion, no compassion. I am not sure that the condition of the church might not be expressed in a phrase I once heard fall from the lips of one who

The Laodicea Letter 197

called himself a Christian. Said he when raising a protest against evangelistic work, with a very evident assumption of superiority and self complacency, " You know, I am thoroughly evangelical but not evangelistic?" Exactly! Tepid. Evangelical but not evangelistic? It is a lie. No man is evangelical without being evangelistic. A man tells me that he is evangelical, that he believes in the ruin of man, and redemption provided by Christ, and in man's responsibility, and yet is not evangelistic! Then he is the worst traitor in the camp of Christ, and that is why Christ hates tepid men and tepid churches. It was that condition that drove John Wesley into the lines of irregular itineracy, which became the regular march of the armies of God. It was that same condition that drove William Booth out into the work of the Christian Mission, which developed into the Salvation Army.

I remember him once telling the story how he was made an enthusiast for salvation. Said he, " I was made a red hot salvationist by an infidel lecturer. That lecturer said, 'If I believed what some of you Christians believe, I would never rest day nor night telling men about it.'" That sentence was the great sentence. William Booth heard, believed, acted.

It was like a fire in his bones, and drove him out from that which was tepid to that which was boiling. Tepid is that condition in which conviction does not affect conscience, heart, or will. The Cross is not denied, but it is not vital. The Cross may have been worn as an ornament, as alas it is too often worn to-day, but these sleek saints had never themselves been nailed to a Cross. The silver cross, the golden Cross worn as an ornament upon the breast creates a pleasant sensation. A wooden cross and iron nails and agonizing death is a different matter. When the Cross is an ornament there is no death in it, but then there is no life in it. When the Cross ceases to be an ornament and becomes the death, then there is a passion that eventuates in contagious life. Sin? Oh certainly the fact of sin was admitted, but there was no hatred of sin. They would speak of sinners as persons to be pitied, but no finger would be lifted to save them. They would speak of sin as something objectionable, perhaps as a moral defect, or an obliquity of vision, but never as a damnable poison, rotting the foundations of life and bringing down into awful cataclasm all fair and lovely things. They were tepid, lukewarm in their creeds and neither cold nor hot

The Laodicea Letter

in their conduct. Is it any wonder that Christ sighed over them "I would thou wert cold or hot."

In the light of this pronouncement the declaration of the church's opinion of itself is terrible. Hear the language as Christ construed it, remembering He was the faithful and true Witness, and this is no exaggeration, but inward conviction. "I am rich," possessing abundantly, "I have gotten riches," the language of perfect self satisfaction, "I have need of nothing," independence.

If we had visited the church at Laodicea in all probability they would have shown us the church premises, they would have told us how much they paid for the property, how much the church cost. They would have said, Whatever we want, we have. If we require new premises, we build them. We are independent. Did you suggest some form of service that would create new spiritual power, they would have been astonished. Did you propose a mission? No, certainly not, we do not want a mission here, we have need of nothing. A series of meetings for the deepening of spiritual life? Oh no, hold them in some other district, we have need of nothing. A time of special humiliation and prayer? We have no need of humiliation, we have need of nothing. That was the condition. They needed nothing because they had everything.

Now listen again. Christ gives His view of their condition. "Thou are the wretched one and miserable and poor and blind and naked."

First, "wretched" and the simple meaning of the word is oppressed with a burden. The burden they carried was the very wealth which they imagined carried them. Instead of wealth helping and lifting them, it hindered and degraded. As He with eyes of fire looked over the churches, of the one that was perhaps the wealthiest, He said it was a heavily burdened one. How different from the popular estimate. We have often heard of a church being heavily burdened with debt, but the Master speaks of one heavily burdened with wealth.

Again "thou art miserable" and the word here means pitiable. The heart of the Lord was moved in pity toward them. He had no congratulation to offer them. His feeling toward them was one of commiseration.

"Thou art poor," and the word means poor as a pauper by the highway side is poor. From His standpoint of wealth the church was a cringing beggar, possessing nothing worth the having.

The Laodicea Letter

"Thou art blind." That is opaque, seeing nothing clearly, seeing nothing afar. Near-sighted is the word which perhaps most accurately expresses the thought, lacking vision, lacking light, devoid of the sense of the far distances, confined within narrow limits.

And "thou art naked," nude, stripped of the clothing of glory and beauty, which ought to adorn the church as the Bride of Jesus Christ. To other churches He has spoken of white raiment. This church has none. Presently the garments of purple, and the jewels of gold will become moth eaten and tarnished, and the church will be seen in the light of the eternities with no robe of purified service to cover it. Let it be specially noted that all these words which Christ uses to describe the church are words of pity. There is not an angry word among them. He is not angry with the condition of the church. All that, He is able to remedy. His anger is that they are satisfied with these things. Read the words yet once again, and note how they pulsate with the pity of His heart.

"Wretched," the condition that ever appeals to the sympathy of the tender-hearted. "Miserable," in such a condition as to touch a sympathetic nature. "Poor," a beggar by the highway side, to whom you can hardly refuse help. "Blind," one groping the way, stretching out hands, that seem to compel you to stretch out yours in guiding kindness. "Naked," making you long to fling some garment of warmth around the denuded form. Such people are saying, We are rich, and have gotten our riches, we do not need anything, and in that very fact lies the deepest note of misery that calls most loudly for a yet deeper compassion. I believe that Christ's attitude to the church was one of profound pity. It was Keith who wrote of this church, "Sooner would a man in Sardis have felt that the chill of death was upon him, and have cried out for life, and called for the physician, than would a man of Laodicea; who would calmly count his even pulse, and think his life secure, when death was preying on his vitals." This is a true picture of Laodicea. "I am rich," "thou art poor;" "I am increased with goods," "thou hast nothing;" "I have need of nothing," "thou are pitiable, blind, naked." Oh the revealing Christ! With what heart-searching does the infinite light of His infinite love fall upon the assemblies of His people.

Now turn to our Lord's counsel to the

The Laodicea Letter

church, and in it even more supremely is His heart revealed.

First, His wish expressed, "I would thou wert cold or hot." Secondly, His declared intention, "I will spew thee out of My mouth." Lastly, His immediate advice, "Buy of Me."

His wish expressed, "I would thou wert cold or hot." Is not that a strange thing for Him to say? We could have understood it better if He had said, "I would thou wert hot." And yet a deep abhorrence of the condition is revealed more forcefully by what He actually said. He would rather have had them cold. There is infinitely greater chance for someone who is cold than for someone who is lukewarm. There is more hope of the man outside the church in all the desolating dreariness of that coldness which is lack of life, and therefore of love, than for the man within the church who is near enough to its warmth not to appreciate it, and far enough away from its burning heat to be useless to God and man. A greater chance for the heathen who has not heard the Gospel than for the man who has become an evangelized heathen, if he disobey the claims of the Evangel. It is impossible to read this epistle without a sense throbbing through the heart of the wail of "I would."

We have heard Him say it before. While yet upon the earth, with a voice full of emotion, as He looked on Jerusalem, He cried, "How often I would have gathered thy children together, . . . and ye would not!" "I would thou wert cold or hot." He would infinitely rather have had to do with a frozen people, clamouring for warmth, than with this crowd of lukewarm rich folk, which having everything had need of nothing, and having nothing had need of everything.

Then follows His declared intention, "I will spew thee out of My mouth," or very literally, "I am about to spew thee out of My mouth." This is not a question of casting a Christian from relation to Himself. It is the casting out of a church from her position of witness bearing. Christ amid the lampstands is speaking to the churches in their capacity of light bearers in the darkness of the night, and He says, I am about to reject thee from this work, about "to spew thee out of My mouth," about to put thee away from the place of witness and testimony. In the form of the statement there is at once a declaration of a decision arrived at, and the intimation of a possible escape from the judgment pronounced. I am about to do it. It is a sentence pronounced,

The Laodicea Letter

it is a doom descending. I am about to do it. It is not yet done. The blow has not fallen. The light is not yet extinguished.

All this lends urgency to the actual words of counsel, as He now utters them, " I counsel thee to buy of Me gold refined by fire, that thou mayest become rich; and white garments that thou mayest clothe thyself, and that the shame of thy nakedness be not made manifest; and eye-salve to anoint thine eyes, that thou mayest see." He now addresses Himself to the church as He sees her, not to the church as she thinks she is, and He confronts her in all fulness as the One possessing all she most sadly lacks, and in His counsel there is a declaration of the way by which all that is objectionable in their condition may be corrected. You are poor, buy My gold, that you may be rich. You are naked, buy My white raiment that you may be clothed. You are blind, buy My eye-salve that you may see. The church says " I am rich, and have gotten riches, and have need of nothing." He says " Thou art miserable and poor and blind and naked." Buy gold from Me that you may be rich. They say We have gotten all we need, and He says You are naked, buy of Me the white garments that you may clothe yourself.

They say We have need of nothing. He says You are blind, buy My eye-salve and anoint your eyes that you may see.

The Lord would teach the church that the true wealth, the true raiment, the true wisdom, the true vision is Himself possessed in all the aspects of His perfection. As Paul had intimated in that letter to the Colossian church, which he desired to be read to the Laodiceans also " that their hearts may be comforted, they being knit together in love, and unto all riches of the full assurance of understanding, that they may know the mystery of God even Christ." If they would be wealthy, they must buy of Him gold refined by fire, they must be rich with what He is. If they would be clothed, it must be with white garments, which are woven out of loyal service rendered to Him, and in the strength of His love. If they would have wisdom they must seek from Him the eye-salve by which they may see things in their true values and perspective. So He approaches the church that He is about to spew out of His mouth in disdain, and opens before them the storehouse of His infinite riches and says If you are only conscious of your poverty, I have riches. If you are but conscious of your nakedness, I have clothing.

The Laodicea Letter

If you are but conscious of your blindness, I have eye-salve. All that can hinder the church will be continuance in the vain delusion that she is rich and increased with goods and has need of nothing. The way back to blessing will be that the church should get down into the dust, into the place of humbling, into the place of heart-break, into the place where she shall indeed say I am poor, and miserable, and blind, and naked. Then He will comfort with His own heart's love, and enrich with His own untold wealth, and clothe with His own white raiment of reward; and anoint with His own inspiration and vision. How graciously He offers to supply the need, and yet with what tender irony mingled with mighty compassion this statement of His ability confronts their false notion of their sufficiency. They said "We are rich." He said "Buy My gold." They said "We have need of nothing." He said Seek all from Me.

Then as in a flash, straight out of His heart of infinite love, comes a statement "As many as I love, I reprove and chasten." If He had not loved the church at Laodicea He would have let her alone. He loved them notwithstanding all their failure, and His love was the reason of His rebuke and of His counsel.

And then words follow, full of a great urgency, "Be zealous and repent." It is as though the Master would do anything to arouse them from their lethargy. He calls them to zeal and to repentance. But how can these people come back? They have not far to travel, though their distance be great, for He is close at hand. Hear the words, the gracious words, "Behold, I stand at the door and knock? if any man hear My voice, I will come in to him, and will sup with him and he with Me." What startling revelations lie within the compass of these words. First, He is excluded. They have everything in the church at Laodicea except Jesus Christ. He is outside the door. We should ever remember that while we have often preached the Gospel from this text, and I do not think it is wrong, that the words are first to the church and not to the individual. "Behold, I stand at the door," the door of the church, "and knock," outside it. Oh, this excluded Christ; excluded from His world, for they crucified Him; excluded from His church, for He is outside the door knocking.

Yet He waits, and for what? For one man to let Him in. He is not waiting for a committee to pass a resolution. Then indeed

The Laodicea Letter

the case might be hopeless. He waits for a man, " If any man hear My voice, I will come in to *him,* and will sup with *him* and *he* with Me." I will first be his Guest " I will sup with him." He shall be My guest, "and he with Me." I will sit at the table which his love provides and satisfy My heart. He shall sit at the table which My love will provide, and satisfy his heart.

Supposing a man in Laodicea opened that door, saying as he did so " I am convinced of our poverty. We have everything but Christ. I will admit Him, and spread the table for Him," what would happen? The moment a man should open the door to Christ, the excluded Christ, and Christ should pass to communion and fellowship with that man, then that man in communion with Christ would excommunicate the church. We have often heard of churches excommunicating men. It is quite possible for one man to excommunicate the church by passing into the place of communion with the Lord. Then how may the church return to fellowship? By joining Christ and that man. Just as the one man came into communication with Christ, so also must the church by including Him Who so long has been excluded. In the Old Testament there is a remarkable illustration of this truth. There was a day when Moses by taking up the tabernacle of the Lord of Hosts, and pitching it without the camp, excommunicated the whole nation from the covenant. To that new centre he called those who sought the Lord into a new position of separation, and as the people returned around that centre in obedience, they were received back into fellowship. There came a day when Christ excommunicated the whole Hebrew nation, and the whole world. It was the day on which He suffered without the camp. Passing outside the camp He rent the veil, and called men to the inner place of worship by calling them back to Himself. Those following Him, entered the Holy of Holies.

So this man in Laodicea who should open the door to Jesus would set up a new standard of life and power, and the only way for the excommunicated church to return would be to take the same position as that man. It is a solemn and awful crisis in the history of a church when in response to the patient calling of the excluded Lord one man shall open the door, and including the Christ, exclude those that have lost their loyalty to Him. There is but one way for such to return, and that is by coming to that man's position.

The Laodicea Letter

We read once in the life story of Jesus of how they excommunicated a man. So angry were they with the testimony that he bore to Jesus, that they cast him out of the synagogue. When Jesus heard of it, He found the man and said "Dost thou believe on the Son of God?" And the man said, "And Who is He, Lord, that I may believe on Him?" And the reply fell with strange strength and sweetness upon the listening ear of that excommunicated man, "Thou hast both seen Him, and He it is that speaketh with thee," and the man said "Lord, I believe, and he worshipped Him." They cast him out of the synagogue the place of worship, but he found the one Centre of worship. It may be that the Laodicean church will exclude the man who includes the Christ. Then let that man have no sorrow in his heart save for the folly of the church. If there be no other way to find Christ than by leaving the Laodicean church then the sooner it be left, the better. To find Him is to find gold refined by fire, and clothing, so that there may be no shame of nakedness, and eyesalve which broadens the outlook, and creates all visions. Oh, behold the vision. Apostasy confront with fidelity, falsehood confront with truth, decorated poverty face to face with infinite wealth, lukewarmness and hypocrisy with compassion and devotion. "Behold, I stand at the door and knock." What dost thou want, oh, crowned One, knocking? A man, one man who will open that I may come in and sup with him, and he with Me.

The last thing to be noticed is a promise to the overcomer. For these people the hardest battle had to be fought, and therefore the greatest reward is promised. The Lord seems to recognize that the difficulty of such life in such a church as Laodicea is the most terrible the saint ever has to fight, and so He makes to them the most gracious and remarkable promise. "He that overcometh, I will give to him to sit down with Me in My throne, as I also overcame, and sat down with My Father in His throne." Beyond this promise neither hope nor imagination can go.

Is there not a suggestion here of the peculiar temptation that Jesus had to meet "as I also overcame?" How did He overcome? What can He mean? A hundred answers come to our thoughts, but do they fit the occasion? There seems to be but one that unlocks the mystery. He is talking to people whose supreme wrong is that they are attempting to take everything easily, they have no compassion, no enthusiasm, and He says to them "Overcome ... as I also overcame." Is there

The Laodicea Letter

not here every evidence of His remembrance of the subtlest temptation that came to Him? The enemy in the wilderness said "All these kingdoms will I give Thee" by an easy way, without the Cross, without the passion, without crucifixion. His own disciple brought to Him the same suggestion, Spare Thyself, what need for all this outpouring of life in a great passion and compassion. And even in Gethsemane we catch the echo of the tempter's voice. I say this with all carefulness, ever remembering that temptation is not sin. I speak only of the echo of temptation as I seem to hear it in His prayer "Father if it be possible, let this cup pass from Me." The enemy was ever saying to Him in one way or another Spare Thyself, why this strenuous life, why set your face like a flint toward Jerusalem, and be determined to tread the via dolorosa? But He overcame, and sat down with His Father in His throne, having taken the only pathway that could issue in the crowning, and now with all the mighty meaning of that fact, He says to the church at Laodicea, to this self-complaisant, self-satisfied, lukewarm, and tepid crowd "Overcome as I also overcame. Be zealous. Be hot, and you shall sit down with Me in My throne."

Very few words are necessary by way of

application of the message of this letter to the age in which we live. The lessons are self evident. I propose to do little more than gather them up, indicating each in brief sentences.

Lukewarmness is in itself a contradiction of all we profess to believe. I do not think in the whole scheme of these letters there is anything of greater importance, or anything more needing emphasis to-day than this truth. The things we profess to believe are of such a nature that we cannot be lukewarm without practically denying them. Better be cold, be frozen. Better abandon all profession of interest in sacred things than to pretend to believe them and sing about them, and yet be lukewarm. We work far more harm to our age by tepid character than by open denial of Christ. It is not the people who are frozen, utterly indifferent, but the people who pretend to love Christ, those, forsooth, who are evangelical, but not evangelistic, who are hindering the progress of His Kingdom. Men who theorize around the atonement, and quarrel over the forms in which they express the truth, and never stretch out the hand to save the lost souls, these are the men who are cursing the Church, men who love to split hairs about election and free will, and yet let the millions drift and do nothing to rescue them. All the wrath of my heart could not equal the words of Christ to such as are lukewarm, "I am about to spew thee out of My mouth." He loathes the unimpassioned regularity of the man who professes to believe the facts which constitute evangelical faith, and does not yield himself to the great claims lying within these truths. Lukewarmness is the worst form of blasphemy. Let the tepid churches call themselves clubs, and we shall know how to deal with them. Let tepid men leave the churches. Let them say they do not believe in Christ for that is the true statement. Let them say there is no sin, for of that position, their actions prove their acceptance. Anything to be rid of the insolent indifference which to Christ and men is calculated cruelty.

And yet another thought, appalling and awful, abides with us as we turn from this study. It is that of the excluded Christ. Oh, how He has suffered, and how He suffers still. Of His own gracious will He was excluded from His heaven for the redemption of lost men; and then excluded from His nation by the blindness of that nation; and then excluded from His world by the apparent victory of the forces of evil. And now, alas, so often excluded from His very Church by the tepid indifference of those who imagine that they have everything while they have nothing.

And yet once more. Oh, the matchless tenderness and patience of this selfsame Son of God. He is the Amen, the faithful and true Witness, the Beginning of the creation of God, and in this letter where He speaks from the standpoint of these primal facts, more than in any other, is revealed the unquenchable love of the heart of God. Insulted, excluded, and ready to spew out of His mouth that which is utterly loathsome, He yet waits, knocking still at the door, willing to enter into new fellowship with one man. To that simply stated fact, nothing that proves tenderness can be added.

Yet we learn, moreover, that the only cure for lukewarmness is the re-admission of the excluded Christ. Apostasy must be confronted with His fidelity, looseness with conviction born of His authority, poverty with the fact of His wealth, frost with the mighty fire of His enthusiasm, and death with the life Divine that is in His gift. There is no other cure for the loneliness of heaven, for the malady of the world, for the lukewarmness of the Church than the readmitted Christ.

The Laodicea Letter

Let us listen to the Son of man as He walks amid the lampstands. Let us beseech Him to say to us all He has to say.

. . . .

What He says to us shall be the truth, for He will preface it with the "I know," and so true will be the statement following that initial word that we shall be compelled to say, This is the word of truth.

. . . .

If He has commendation for us, the uttering of it shall be our chief reward. If He speak words of complaint, heeding them, let us find our way to true and deep repentance.

. . . .

Let us listen principally for His words of counsel, and hearing them without reserve let us yield to Him our quick obedience.

. . . .

He also says to all the churches, "I will." It is the word of His judgment. It is the word of His promise. This we know, that what He wills is best, so to His chastisements we render ourselves that we may find His great reward.

. . . .

"He that hath an ear, let him hear what the Spirit saith to the churches."

www.ingramcontent.com/pod-product-compliance
Lightning Source LLC
Chambersburg PA
CBHW071441150426
43191CB00008B/1188